Women, Relationships, & Kabbalah

Questions & Answers
about
Women's Spiritual Fulfillment

Women, Relationships, & Kabbalah

Questions & Answers
about
Women's Spiritual Fulfillment

Laitman
Kabbalah
Publishers

By Rav Michael Laitman PhD

WOMEN, RELATIONSHIPS, & KABBALAH
Questions & Answers About Women's Spiritual Fullfilment

Copyright 2014 by MICHAEL LAITMAN
All rights reserved

Published by Laitman Kabbalah Publishers
www.kabbalah.info www.kab.tv
1057 Steeles Avenue West, Suite 532, Toronto, ON, M2R 3X1, Canada
2009 85th Street #51, Brooklyn, New York, 11214, USA

Printed in Canada

*The contents were compiled and edited by students of Dr. Michael
Laitman according to their understanding of the material.

Library of Congress Control Number: 2014910748

ISBN: -978-1-897448-96-0

Content Editors: Debbie Sirt, Debbie Wood
Editing: Mary Penock
Review: Norma Livne
Executive Editor: Chaim Ratz
Research: Zhanna Allen, Veronica Edwards, Brenda Jones, Leah
Goldberg, Susan Morales-Kosinec, Judy Hobart, Nina Chulak.
Layout: Rony Perry
Cover: Inna Smirnova
Publishing and Post Production: Uri Laitman

FIRST EDITION: DECEMBER 2014
First printing

Contents

Introduction 1

Love According to Kabbala 2

Condition of Love 2

Concerning Love 3

Relationships between
Men and Women 5

Choosing a Partner 8

Investing in Each Other 10

Husband and Wife:
Where Is the Creator between Them? 11

The Companion Chosen
for Me by the Creator 12

Connecting All the Worlds 13

Don't Let Us Down! 14

Kabbalah on Sex 15

The Reason for Embarrassment 17

Marriage 18

Maintaining a Successful Relationship 20

Equality between Men and Women 22

A Place Deserving of a Woman 22

In Spirituality Everyone Is Equal 24

Jealousy 24

Today, It's Spiritual Relationship or
no Relationship 25

A Partner Who Does Not Study 26

Questions from Women Whose Husbands
Don't Study Kabbalah 27

The Nature and Role of Women in Kabbalah.................................29

The Importance of Women in Kabbalah.................................29

The Nature of Women and How It Differs
from That of Men.................................30

The Roles of Women and How They Differ
from Those of Men.................................30

Inner Work of a Woman.................................31

Seen Others as Corrected.................................31

The Most Efficient Way to Aim
toward the Goal.................................31

Correction of a Woman's Soul.................................33

The Root of a Woman's Soul,
and How Does It Differ From a Man's.................................33

A Woman Is More Corrected and Closer
to Nature than a Man.................................33

A Woman's Greatest and Deepest Desire.................................34

Women Crossing the Machsom.................................35

How a Woman Knows She Is Advancing Sufficiently
and Correctly.................................36

The Ways to Approach the Creator.................................37

Can a Woman's Soul Reincarnate
in the Body of a Man, or Vice Versa?.................................38

The Women's Desire as the
Engine of Creation.................................39

A Convention That Will Ignite the Flame
in Our Hearts.................................40

Wake Up the Men!.................................41

Woman Is Where Changes Take Place.................................42

Be More Insolent With the Creator.................................43

Unify to Give Birth to the Creator..43

Help Me Cope With Men!..44

Unity..46

A Letter to the Beloved in the Front..46

Don't Wait, Act!..47

The Women's Group Is Beyond Hierarchies..48

Women's Work along Two Lines..49

Convergence of Two Desires..50

Women's Questions in Preparation
for the Convention..51

Women Will Succeed!..54

The Women's Convention: Rising Above
the Imaginary Show..54

Actions on the Home Front Prepare the Weapon
for the Attack in the Desert..56

The Unified Women's Desire..57

The Ideal Women's Unity..58

To Break through the Cocoon
and Enter the Spiritual World..58

Family Relationships..60

Balancing Home, the Outside World,
and Kabbalah..61

Everything Requires a Skill..62

Children..64

Teaching Children Kabbalah..64

The Role of Women in Nurturing Their Children
with Respect to Kabbalah..69

The Father's Role in Educating His Children
in Kabbalah..71

When Parents Disagree on the Need to Educate
Their Children in Kabbalah..73

The Best and Most Correct Environment
for a Child...73

Should a Child Be Isolated
or Sheltered in Any Way?..79

Group..80

Women's Desire Leads...80

The Most Reliable Thing in the World..80

The Thin Line between Male
and Female Work..81

Don't Confuse the Spiritual
with the Physical..83

High Hopes...84

No Development without Women..85

Behind Every Successful Man
There Is a Woman..87

One Global Woman and One Global Man..87

Who Smoothes Conflicts in the Group?..88

Men, Do Not Underestimate
the Desire of Women!..88

Women's Participation Is Crucial...90

The Mother's Way...91

Wiping Out the Differences
in Spiritual Work..92

The Unity of the World Lies in Harmony
between Men and Women..93

Dissemination..96

Dissemination and Unity...96

Introduction

The questions presented here are simply the clothing for the deep longing that we all feel.

In the answers, may we be reminded of our important role in bringing all of humanity to the fulfillment of the purpose of creation.

The study of Kabbalah is the study of the relationship between the vessel and the light and how to transform this inner opposition into one of mutual support, a shared embrace consisting of the singular force of love.

Our relationships in this world reflect the underlying structure and goal of nature, and once a person feels the need to be in harmony with this goal, their relations become the medium by which they can measure their progress.

The sages tell us that the corrected connection between us amounts to the same thing as the revelation of the Creator. This is because the appearance of a sincere desire to connect with and serve all people as if they were our own family, spouse, or child, is none other than the divine quality itself. This is how the Upper Force treats us, and this is what we must reach.

But this isn't a path we walk alone. We put in efforts together and receive attainment only as a united desire. Our point of greatest need, connection and the maximum attraction of the reforming Light occur in the morning lesson. In these hours we truly come together as a single creature to enter the flow of Light that may pass through us to the world. This flow is the real news of the day and the real sustenance of humanity.

Love According to Kabbala

...What is "love" in our world? It's when something awakens a feeling in me that I might get pleasure from it. I then aspire to this thing, to this spark of Light. I want to get closer to this Light and connect to it, so it will fulfill me. The pleasure can come from food, sex, family, money, power, or knowledge. But what do I really connect to? I connect to the spark of pleasure that enters my desire for pleasure. This is what "love" in our world is.

...True love is when you fulfill the desires of another as if they are your own. This means that you love your neighbor rather than yourself. It is when you work with and fulfill his desire. This is love for one's neighbor.

Condition of Love

...I call my attitude to something that brings me pleasure "love." I love coffee; therefore I drink it. I feel pleasure when I do this. This means that I love it. In other words, I love the pleasure that is in coffee. This is not the love we are discussing. You use this word for a completely different sensation and attitude to an object.

Love is not reception of pleasure from somebody; it is giving to the object of love...

...In Kabbalah love has a very capacious scientific definition. Speaking briefly and approximately, it is when a person can feel someone else's inner world, his desires, needs, and serves to fulfill him. The sensation that he feels while fulfilling another is called "love." At the same time, he himself feels delighted.

There is no love in our world. What we call love is the aspiration for pleasure, or to be fulfilled by pleasure. In other words, corporeal love is one's attitude to that which gives one pleasure. It is measured by the degree of one's fulfillment from the source of love.

Spiritual love works differently. It's when a person rises above his egoism and no longer depends on it. He then begins to perceive the desires of others as his own, and unites with the entire desire that was created by the Creator (with the common soul, *Adam*).

...When speaking of the realm of this world where we all meet in the meantime, love certainly cannot exist beyond personal gain. When we turn to the people who occupy themselves with the nature of man, they will tell us it is all only hormones, habits, calculations, and no more. Even the mother who loves her little son is, after all, acting out of her inner urges, out of natural love. Should we disconnect her love for her son, she would then have no more love for him than she has for her neighbor's child. Based on natural instinct, she does not think of her neighbor's child, but constantly thinks of her own because nature commits her to love him.

It is the same with partners. When two people meet and are interested in one another, it is similar to the "love of fish," which means one loves the other because he is useful to me. I have some lust or benefit in our meeting. This is called loving him, though actually it is the love of what I can receive from him. In fact, I am exploiting him. There can be no other kind of relation in our world, in our life.

Concerning Love

Question:
Can you give a Kabbalistic explanation of the feeling of love?

Dr. Laitman:
...Kabbalah says that the greatest pleasure in the world is the perception of union with the Creator. Our earthly love is merely a weak reflection of this higher love...

Question:

*What are the objective reasons for the emergence of this feeling –
love?*

Dr. Laitman:

Love in our world and in the Kabbalistic world is a specific
reaction to pleasures...

Our most common love for anything emerges because the object
we love contains pleasure, some kind of Light or even micro-
dose of Light.... This object may be kids, the opposite sex or
delicious food...

Relationships between Men and Women

...[S]cientists assert that all the inner relations between man and woman determine how society develops. This is because the man develops so as to look good in the eyes of a woman, and the woman develops in such a way so as to connect to the man and elicit the right reaction from him. Whether we understand it or not, it is within our genes and we calculate our actions accordingly. These inner most deep, ancient and natural drives cannot be removed. However, if we used them correctly, knowing what exists within us and dominates us, we would be able to arrange our lives more favorably.

Question:

What expression does this difference find in spiritual development?

Dr. Laitman:

The wisdom of Kabbalah explains that the root of the soul of man and that of the woman are totally different. They are opposite and complement one another. It also explains the development of the soul of man and that of woman by different powers, systems, processes and orders.

However, though they appear different, they complement each other at every level. They must have contact and mutually complement one another so that each is complete. Man must receive from the woman what he lacks, and the woman must receive from the man what she is deficient in. With this mutual influence they reach the final correction. It is not possible to reach *Elokim*, which is the power of oneness in nature, if these two do not unite. As it is written, "The Divine presence dwells between man and woman."

Therefore, Kabbalah speaks of the mutual correction, explains our foundations, how to reach completion, and through it achieve the best possible state that can be in all worlds. When we come to know and execute the mutual correction, we will reach completion. Herein lies the solution to the problems we see today such as children detached from their families, alienation of couples, divorces and more.

...However, even in our world the relationships between the sexes where the male part is "bestowing" and the female part is "receiving" are ambiguous. Even psychologists assert that everything men accomplish in this world, they accomplish only in order to ultimately assert themselves in the eyes of women. This way, with its seeming external weakness, the woman's part compels the man's part to work hard in order to win and throw what it has won to the woman's feet...

...Men and women's souls come from different spiritual sources, and therefore incarnate into our world in such different creatures. All the differences between the sexes are caused precisely by souls, as well as differences in types and sub-types, classes and sub-classes of all creations...

...A man's entire pride consists in the fact that he is able to bring something to a woman and give to her. He thinks that he wins her heart by doing this.

We can see that even in our world, despite everything, men and women have naturally different functions. Is there anything higher than the act of birth? It is an act equivalent to creation or equivalence to the Creator!

In reality, a woman's nature is a very good one. After all, a woman's ultimate necessity is to be given the opportunity to express love. She wants to have a man that will be able to apprehend the self-expression of her love and her desire to be loved...

...Men are not ready for this; it is part of being uncorrected...

The difference between man and woman in our world is the consequence of the relationship between the male and female parts of the soul. In our world we can see that men and women perceive the world around them differently, and have different responsibilities and tasks. In the spiritual world, the male and female parts of the *Partzuf* or soul complement each other. The female part gives her desires and the male part gives his screens. Ultimately, there emerges a mutual revelation of the Light or Creator, meaning attainment. Together they comprise perfection.

...[T]o this the feminine part is the receiver, while the masculine part is the one that produces the similarity to the Creator out of itself. The masculine part generates Light, and the feminine part is the recipient of this Light. However, naturally the masculine part is not able to raise its desires to the corresponding level, without the feminine part, because it does not have the same sharpness of desires because of the lack of realization that the feminine part has.

Question:
What does it mean that a woman complements the man in the same way his mother does?

Dr. Laitman:
Man needs warmth, a home, all that belongs to a family. He was used to getting this from his mother, and now he gets a part of this from his wife.

Everything occurring in our world is the result of the Upper Force's influence that descends to our world. In order to really understand what is happening, it is necessary to study the Upper Forces, their attributes, predestination and purpose.

...It may seem to us that the difference between the sexes is merely external and hormonal and that we can make a man into a woman in a purely medicinal way by using surgery and hormone replacement. However, the difference is much deeper and it lies in the very root of the universe, in our souls' roots. The difference comes from there and precisely we, men and women, have different types of souls.

The difference between man and woman in our world is the consequence of the relationship between the male and female parts of the soul. In our world we can see that men and women perceive the world around them differently, and they have different responsibilities and tasks.

In the spiritual world the male and female parts of the *Partzuf* or soul complement each other. The female part gives her desires and the male part gives his screens. Ultimately, there emerges a mutual revelation of the Light or Creator, meaning attainment. Together they comprise perfection.

...Man and woman are the embodiment of the relationships between *Zeir Anpin* and *Malchut* of the world of *Atzilut*. Their connection's essence and level give a specific name to a level. Masculine and feminine states are constant states on all 125 spiritual levels.

Choosing a Partner

Question:
...What attributes should I look for in a man? And is there such a thing as a soul mate? Someone who complements me? Is there something mystical that I should be searching for? Or simply a good man who will be a good provider, a good father, one who I am a little attracted to. How does a single woman today look for a man? We see that she is unsuccessful in finding one. Why?

Dr. Laitman:
Because society has confused them, and they are looking for standards that the society tells them about. They are looking for someone macho, brilliant in something, a smooth talker or

something, but not according to what their own nature tells them that they need.

There is a law of all the reality of all nature in general, both spiritual and corporeal. It is called, "The law of equivalence." Also on the mental level, physiology, psychological, on all levels: inanimate, vegetative, animate, speaking, it doesn't matter where or what, the more one is similar to the other, the more successful.

Question:
They succeed?

Rav Laitman:
They succeed more.

Question:
Oh, don't opposites attract?

Dr. Laitman:
No. Opposites attract only to play and fool around. But not more than that.

Question:
But for stability in couples, is it preferred that they be similar in attributes...?

Dr. Laitman:
... "To find" [a partner] is called to develop herself.

In this world we find ourselves in a huge field of powers, let's say, magnetic power. And we are attracted with our inner potential, which is like an electrical charge, to this place where she feels there is something opposing her. If a woman develops her personality a little more, then she feels how far off she is from where this personality is that exactly suits her...

Question:

...So actually our message to men and women is if you connect to yourself at the correct and true level, then you...

Dr. Laitman:

...At an internal level. You won't be mistaken; you will find the correct relationship that will be successful...

Investing in Each Other

...It is necessary to ponder about the relationship between the sexes in order to fully understand that one has absolutely no advantage over the other, that they both achieve perfection only by completing each other. They accomplish this by satisfying the condition that each one fulfills its own function.

...To the degree we become equivalent to the common echelon, the Creator, we are able to love each other as parts of one whole, or the single common Soul. We acquire the ability to see our true companion, both the spiritual companion and the physical or earthly one. Together we will really be able to perceive the full union to the degree of our spiritual ascent.

Nothing brings a man and woman closer than mutual study of Kabbalah. There is a reason for the saying, "Husband and wife - the *Shechina* is between them."

The *Shechina* is the Divine presence. According to my teacher's advice, I encourage couples to mutually study at home. We have accepted this as a constant practice. Therefore, many of our families can brag about having the perception of love. We wish you to have the same.

Husband and Wife:
Where Is the Creator between Them?

Question:

Please elaborate on the type of connection in a family of which it is written: "Husband and wife, and the Creator (Shechina) between them."

My Answer:

This means that I want any connection between the two of us to be actualized through the Upper Force that I wish to regard my spouse as a partner given to me by the Creator. It's just like Adam asked after his transgression: "Was it not You who had given me this woman?" Therefore, in a man's attitude toward his wife dwells the Creator, and this is something we will yet reveal.

If a husband and wife are interconnected, this becomes a powerful means for revealing the Creator. It is a great fortune if a person is provided this field of work. And one doesn't need a lot of time to realize it, only a few minutes a day. The rest of the time he has to devote to the group and the study.

Every connection transpires on its own level, but they are all united in that their sole purpose is to reveal the Creator. With respect to the friends in the group, we want the Creator to dwell among us. Herein lies the purpose in unifying into a group as well as a family. These are the different levels of connection with the same *Shechina*, and everybody who exists on the other side of Her (my wife, the group, the friends, and the whole world) are, in fact, parts of my own soul.

Regarding a wife, it is written that the Creator took a part of the man's soul and made a helper against him. Similarly, the entire world is set against me as a result of the breaking as "help against me." All this is part of my soul as well. Presently, I feel all this as external and separate from me, but thanks to the *Shechina* and the

Creator's presence, it all merges for me into a single whole. If I draw the Upper Light, the Creator, the middle line, He will unite all of it into one.

If we examine where the deepest and soundest connection is made – between a husband and wife, the friends in the group, all of humanity, or the entire universe – the innermost connection is found between a husband and wife.

The Companion Chosen for Me by the Creator

Question:

Is there a difference in the spiritual development of women and men, and what constitutes this difference?

Answer:

If we look at the historical process, we see that as soon as Abraham began to reveal the wisdom of Kabbalah, he received an order to adhere with his female part: "Listen to what Sarah tells you." Everything is determined by the female part. What a man reveals is revealed by him in the woman, meaning the male part of the soul in the inner female part of the soul and the man in the woman. Rabash wrote and spoke repeatedly about the fact that in the corrected society, in a corrected family with a man and a woman, the husband and a wife are in the process of revealing the Creator between them. The husband perceives the wife through the Creator and the wife relates to the husband in the same manner. They constantly feel that the Creator dwells between them. That is, I know that I received her from the Creator. And if I perceive her as a part that can help me reach the Creator, then I am truly realizing myself.

Question cont.:

In other words, my wife is my partner on the spiritual path?

Answer:

She is not just a partner. I see her as a companion chosen for me by the Creator. And if I treat her this way, I don't just address her. I address her and the Creator at the same time and feel that she relates to me in the same manner. It seems like an unnatural contrast, but it is very natural because it is very goal-oriented. It turns out that at every moment of my life, from the most intimate to the most common situations in the family, and even more so in public and in the world, we begin to treat each other like the Creator dwells between us. We feel that this Force needs to bind us together, fill the voids between us, and correct the rejection and hatred that rises up between us. The Creator Himself comes to fill this space and unite us with each other. We can begin to realize this in the family, the closest place for every person, and continue it throughout the whole world.

Connecting All the Worlds

Question:

Is a man's wife one of the "neighbors" or "friends" who he needs to "love as himself?"

Answer:

Our life in this world is arranged so that we have to connect for the sake of the spiritual goal in our families, too. This is a consequence of the highest and brightest spiritual root, and it applies to every person in the world.

As a result of the breaking, our souls have separated and become opposite to one another. This applies not only to the "man – Creator" or "group – Creator," but also to the "husband – wife" pair. We have come to the stage of the breaking of the family unit, so spouses, too, will have to realize the principle of "Love thy neighbor as thyself."

It works between a husband and wife the same way as towards other people. And when a husband and wife will merit this connection, Shechina, the Creator, will dwell between them. This means that in all their actions from the most material to the most spiritual one, they will strive to remain in one intention: to be connected only through mutual bestowal, the Creator.

Every person can reveal this, and this is precisely why the Creator divided the first man into two parts: Adam and Eve. This opportunity is already preset in every married couple in this world. I am convinced that we must correct this area. After all, until we bring all the corrections to their completion on the lowest degree, the corrections won't exist Above either.

It is not enough to feel like we are connected. In this world, we have to connect in all our material things in a perfect form, like in the World of Infinity. And then these two vertexes, our world and the World of Infinity, will connect and everything will return to its perfect state. We need to connect these two worlds: the highest one and the lowest one.

For this reason, everything needs to be happening in accordance with the spiritual laws, both in family life and in one's attitude toward children and adults. And, of course, when a husband and wife both study Kabbalah and are able to reach this kind of attitude and intention toward one another, this reveals opportunities to do one of a kind work that is possible only with a spouse.

Don't Let Us Down!

Question:

I want to understand what the secret of the Kazakhstan Group is. They always radiate joy and they always impress me. I spoke to one of the women from that group and she told me: "I have a strong husband!" In other words, she has no doubt that he will not do anything wrong or may get off track; it simply amazes me! Could it be that the women are the secret?

Answer:

Unfortunately, I don't know these women, but apparently they are right. When a woman speaks about her husband that way it gives him great support! The main thing for men, even for the toughest macho man, is a woman's support. He needs it very much. When a woman speaks this way about her husband, he cannot allow himself to be weak. He will do everything in his power to justify her opinion so as not to seem lesser in her eyes.

A clever woman knows that, uses that, and benefits from that. A woman can help her husband that way much more than the whole group since she is part of her husband. If she supports him, his success is guaranteed.

So women, take into account that this special mission is in your hands. The female part and the male part are internally connected to one another by natural ties that we don't know about. They are transferred by inner reflection from us to you and vice versa.

Your influence on us is great and you can determine the men's success. I really count on you. Don't let us down!

Kabbalah on Sex

Dr. Laitman:

...Yes, it is indeed the biggest desire, i.e. the desire for sex. This is the way nature arranged it because our continuation depends on that. And if a person had no desire for that, then maybe he wouldn't even connect to it. Animals go according to their inner programming. Besides that, in spirituality it is the highest pleasure, the pleasure of *Zivug* (mating), i.e., the *Zivug* with the Creator. It is not a pleasure through all kinds of external coverings.

It is said that of all the spiritual pleasure only a small spark of it descended down to our world. And that small spark clothes itself in all kinds of coverings, in food, sex, children, in sweet, in hot, in all kinds of things—in things that seem to me that there is pleasure in them. What awakens the strongest in me, according to man's nature, is the pleasure of sex.

Question:

Let's say that they arrange a partner for me who is a pilot, or doctor, etc, but as to the physical attraction, he repulses me. According to my intelligence I know that he is suitable for me and will be a good partner, but what about simple, sexual, physical attraction?

Dr. Laitman:

It is very important. If the partner is physically repulsive, it is impossible to overlook it. The Torah also talks about it and it is forbidden to do it. It is forbidden to go against nature.

Question:

You wouldn't advise it even though this person has exactly all the attributes that I have been looking for all my life, but I am just not attracted to him?

Dr. Laitman:

No, I wouldn't advise it. So his qualities are all Right, and sometimes you even feel some kind of lofty feelings, and then afterwards you fall into regular life. If the person near you repulses you, there is nothing you can do.

Question:

Originally, Adam had only one woman, Eve. Will we return to monogamy when corrected? Or will we not care when we are corrected?

Dr. Laitman:

Sexual union in our world comes from the spiritual union

between the Upper Light and the soul, called *"Zivug de Hakaa"* by means of a screen. In this spiritual union between the soul and the Creator (the *Kli* and the Light), the Creator or the Light is the male part that bestows, and the soul or *Kli* is the female part that receives. In the process of correction, the soul *(Kli)* acquires the property of bestowal, and then it is ready to accept the Light in order to satisfy the Creator's (the Light's) desire "to bestow."

The process of union (merging, *Zivug* - spiritual coupling) happens in the common desires of both "to fulfill the other with pleasure," to feel pleasure only to the extent that will give pleasure to the other partner. Hence, what happens is a constant comparison of common desires and intentions (in the Rosh of the *Partzuf*, before reception inside its *Toch*), which becomes expressed in our physiology as the movements of sexual intercourse, preceding the outpouring of the *Light of Hochma (Ohr Pnimi*, semen) into the soul (into the *Kli*, from the Rosh into the *Toch* of the Partzuf). These alternating and progressive mutual movements are meant to create a complete desire in each spiritual partner, by way of interrupting and resuming contact. This creates the possibility of wholesome pleasure: when this level is attained, the Light passes from *Peh* to *Toch* - the pleasure enters the desire, as written in the Torah: "As an arrow hits the desired target at the desired time, in the desired woman, and in the desired place."

Thus, when one's soul attains full correction, one views sex as the physiological expression of the spiritual connection. And if there is no spiritual connection, then there is no incentive or reason for a bodily connection.

The Reason for Embarrassment

Question:

If we say that sex is a natural phenomenon, then why are there embarrassment, restrictions, and awkwardness around this issue?

Why are people generally ashamed to talk about sex, if it also has a spiritual root?

Rav Laitman:

It is very interesting to see this on the example from the Bible: Adam and Eve suddenly discovered that they were naked (they had not noticed that previously). They began to feel embarrassed about their nakedness and made clothes for themselves. Everything started from this. Animals do not feel embarrassed; they just fight for coupling, no more than that. This is where the difference between the animate and human level manifests in the first place.

This is because a human being already feels freedom of will, choice in his actions, in unity with this or that possible partner, in this or that quality of such unity. Since his freedom of will manifests here, a person feels embarrassed. He chooses the quality of his actions, how this can be regarded in the eyes of others, what result this may bring, etc. In other words, everything that refers to sex as well as reception of pleasure in any more or less noticeable portions at the human level has to do with awkwardness. This is because a person can choose how to act. If these actions of ours were not free, but strictly determined by nature, then we would have no special attitude toward them. We would fulfill our functions just like animals do.

Marriage

Question:

What is marriage?

Dr. Laitman:

Marriage is the interaction of two absolutely different and opposite parts of creation.

Generally, marriage is the connection of the Creator and creation, in which the Creator is the male part and creation is the female part.

Although creation is initially absolutely opposite to the Creator, it must enter into full union with the Creator by gradually becoming closer to Him. This absolutely complete final union, or the state when creation fully unifies with the Upper Force, is called "marriage."

With correspondence to what we must spiritually do with our souls, the same thing occurs with us on Earth between man and woman as a result of our historical development. It takes place as an imprint or copy of spiritual events or actions.

If we knew the spiritual roots and the rules of behavior between these roots, meaning the attributes of these roots, then we would be able to really take pleasure in the earthly marriage in our world or create a perfect connection and unbound happiness.

Since people do not know the upper root, we are drowning in constant suffering. Marriage is losing its necessity in general, because people are discovering the impossibility of any connection within marriage.

However, if people knew how to create their relationships in equivalence to spiritual roots, then any man and woman would have a perfect connection in the same way this exists in the Upper World. They would be happy, honest and would complement each other, based on knowledge of their own spiritual root and the spiritual root of their spouse. In this case marriage would be ideal. Over the course of their lives, spouses would achieve their spiritual roots and carry out their predestination.

There is a simple solution, explained in the Bible very simply. It is written: "Husband and wife, *Shechina* (the presence of the Creator) between them." If we introduce a certain binding element—called *Shechina*—between husband and wife, then they really can be husband and wife; that is, they can unite with each other.

What does this binding element represent? It comes into existence when both partners go beyond their egoism, beyond their desire for delight. By doing this, they also turn into a single *Kli*, in which *Shechina* reigns. Their sensation in this common *Kli* is called love.

Basically, love is a joint sensation of the Creator, who delves inside of a common *Kli* between the two people who love each other, and it cannot manifest itself in any other form.

...If a human being advances and attains the degree of love of the Creator, and in addition, he has a wife with whom he can work with in the same manner, then of course, as they advance, they create between each other a system of *Kelim*, a connection in which they feel the Light existing between them.

...If his friend or wife participates in his work for the Creator, they start building their joint *Kelim*. There is a difference between building joint *Kelim* among the friends in the group and building joint *Kelim* with one's wife.

The difference is huge and essential. The type of *Kelim* that a Kabbalist creates with his wife resembles the Supreme bond (*Zivug*) between the Creator and all the created beings, between the Creator and the souls of *Adam ha Rishon*, or between the Creator and all the souls. In these *Kelim*, in this bond, the unique revelation of the relationship and connection is taking place; the connection and relationship between the Creator and all created beings is felt in such bond.

Maintaining a Successful Relationship

Question:

Why is it that before we find our match, we have to go through so much pain and disappointment?

Dr. Laitman:

It is because you use the wrong criteria to look for a partner. Your spouse should be someone you understand, someone similar to you, with a similar upbringing and childhood, and you should remind him of his mother. Everything else will fall into place throughout the process of living together. Mostly, it will happen when you forgive one another and compromise with each other.

Question:

There is a couple starting out their relationship. Both study Kabbalah. They now have the opportunity to create the right connection between them. How should this occur? How can they aim their relationship toward the goal?

Dr. Laitman:

Tune into the studies together, discuss them, and read articles together. This is what Rabash advised for couples.

Question:

In one of your talks about relationships, you said that when a couple has a disagreement about something, the best thing to do is keep quiet and not argue, and this silence will lead to a new understanding of one another and a new level in your relationship. You will also set an example for your partner. Can you please talk about this some more? This is a sore spot in my relationship, and I think that there are many couples going through this.

Dr. Laitman:

Staying silent in an argument, compromising, causes your partner to react in the same way. Compromising leads to union and understanding, an understanding that we need to unite over our egoism. In such a way, we develop respect for one another, even for each other's weaknesses, and understanding of each other's nature, and this, in turn, leads to love, regardless of the obvious uncorrected properties of each partner. It says in King David's Psalms: "Love covers all sins!" That is, the sins still remain, but the two of you learn to rise over them and unite there.

Equality between Men and Women

Question:

Should the relationship between men and women be traditional as it was in the past when it comes to dividing up the roles?

Dr. Laitman:

I think that in today's modern society the roles cannot be divided in the way it was possible long ago, where the kitchen belonged to the woman and the garage belonged to the man... the division should be done freely in each and every family... when we start talking about dividing up the roles, what each one owes, then this is not good as it is opposite to collaboration. If, instead of doing this, we worry about unity between us, then our unity that is correctly reciprocated will always be part of things correctly.

Question:

I see many couples around me who seem to be living together but somehow separately. There is nothing connecting them besides a primitive household. How does Kabbalah explain the connection between a man and woman?

Dr. Laitman:

Kabbalah says that love between people can exist only through the Creator. It is said, "Husband and wife, the *Shechinah* (perception of the Creator) is between them." This is the same as "Love your neighbor as yourself." It is possible only if it is bound by the Creator's existence and His governance from above. Otherwise, there is nothing binding and nothing that evokes any feeling of bestowal.

A Place Deserving of a Woman

Our world is egoistic. Everything here is based on egoism, authority, status, and power. That's why a woman plays a secondary role in this world.

A man enjoys more power and independence than a woman. He is not as attached to his house or children. He conquers space, discovers continents; his imagination and enthusiasm are stronger, and he is more passionate in playing games. Men go "wild" in this world.

A woman, by nature, is more moderate and represents a more serious force. She balances out this world, and embodies the power of a household and family. From the point of view of continuation of the human race, she is the most important part of nature.

But since our world is egoistic and aggressive, men who possess strength, freedom, and ability to break through to the top usually hold positions that they don't deserve. Consequently, they define many things in this world, whereas women treat them with lenience and compliance.

This applies to everything: religion, science, everyday life, career advancement, and salary. Men leave to women only those places that they are not interested in. This is how unfairly our egoistic world is built.

But the wisdom of Kabbalah speaks about a totally different (reverse) reality where everything is governed by the force of bestowal and love that evens out all dissimilarities and contradictions. We have to give weight to everything which is worthy of it. This is what nature, harmony, and perfection demand from us, not to mention the wisdom of Kabbalah.

If we transition from receiving to bestowal, we will see a reverse world in which a woman (*Malchut* which translates as "Kingdom") occupies an essential place. She is the one who rules!

It is derived from the structure of the spiritual worlds. A woman (*Malchut*) is positioned in the core of all the worlds, and everything there is exists only for her sake since she is the one who gives birth and develops a new world.

That's why only with the help of the wisdom of Kabbalah a woman can reach her genuine purpose and attain an adequate and fair status that she naturally deserves.

In Spirituality Everyone Is Equal

Question:

When I am sitting in a circle with other women, are they my group? Should I attach my thoughts to the men's part during a women's workshop?

Answer:

Why do you have to think about the men? It does not matter whether it is a man or woman in front of you. They are the friends with whom you are communicating now. And if we could cross out the gender and not see this division? In front of me is just a desire, and this desire transmits its thoughts to me. Then, there would be no problem at all.

I do not believe that women can understand spiritual matters less than men can. If they really want to raise themselves, they can do this, but they have another problem: For some reason, they think they are incapable. This pushes them down.

Jealousy

Question:

What is jealousy from the point of view of Kabbalah? Does this feeling have a spiritual explanation?

Dr. Laitman:

...All of this can be explained by biologists, geneticists, and botanists.

Question:

About pistils and stamens?

Dr. Laitman:

Yes. Plants, insects, and people - all function under the influence of hormones. These are inner biological processes, and we should not pass them off as love.

The problem is that man is not sufficiently developed in order to understand that his inner world is a world of pleasure! If he enjoys a beautiful picture, music, a woman, a child, a soup - it is all the same! If he receives pleasure while being as he was born and brought up, then this is called egoistical enjoyment.

Love is based on giving, on transcending oneself; whereas the processes occurring within us are purely animate. For some reason, we pass some of them off as unreal feelings and demand the same from others. What kind of love is this? You will receive an injection of hormones and you will treat the object of your love in a totally different way. This is pure chemistry.

Today, It's Spiritual Relationship or no Relationship

Today, it is practically impossible for a man and a woman to maintain a good relationship over time, unless there is a spiritual connection between them. It's because their egos clash and destroy their connection. Today, there are countless divorces, and most relationships fall apart because our egos are "on fire," and they only grow bigger with time. The beautiful verse, "Man, woman, and the Divine Presence between them," simply does not exist in such couples.

So what does it take to create that spiritual connection between them, the only thing that can remedy their relationship? Having a spiritual connection means that both partners know the reason for their existence: to embark on the spiritual journey and attain the spiritual goal of life. Then they will have something that truly connects them, they will be in a mutual "cell" together, and the verse, "Man, woman, and the Divine Presence between them," will really come true. In other words, they will feel the revelation of the Divine Presence, the Creator.

In accordance with spiritual roots, if man were to fulfill his foremost mission—self-correction—and would do the same with regard to his wife and kids, meaning if he were to inject a spiritual element into the relationship between them all, then according to the spiritual roots of being in such relationship, his woman would demand of him nothing more.

A Partner Who Does Not Study

Question:

I began to study Kabbalah, and I would like my husband to study as well, but his interests are completely different. What can I do?

Dr. Laitman:

Leave him alone.

Question:

A woman becomes fulfilled spiritually through a man - I feel this very clearly. However, all I can think about is my boyfriend, who doesn't study Kabbalah. I broke up with him when I encountered Kabbalah, but now we are back together and I am still studying Kabbalah. I feel like I prefer spending time with him over going to the lessons, and this scares me because I'm neglecting my purpose and the Creator's goal for me. I can't leave you and the group and the entire world Kli. I need you and you need me. But on the other hand, I am drawn to my boyfriend. I really want to be on the path and develop my Kli together with a man, but I feel like I wouldn't be able to manage without my boyfriend.

Dr. Laitman:

If he loves you then he won't interfere with your Kabbalah studies.

Questions from Women Whose Husbands Don't Study Kabbalah

Dr. Laitman:

If the husband doesn't want to study Kabbalah, it is forbidden to pressure him. Maybe the time hasn't come, and before it does he needs to act like a regular person.

Of course, we can give him a newspaper to read or a little book, or explain a little bit to him. However, while wanting to draw his interest toward the science of Kabbalah, we need to treat him softly and nicely, without forcing him to do anything and without any disdain. Otherwise, we simply push the person away.

On the contrary, when he begins to take a slight interest in Kabbalah, the woman should use all her strength to show him that she is ready to do anything for him just so he would study and be connected to this. She will love him, forgive him for everything, respect and value him just as long as he studies. The man will buy into this, since we know how much a man wants to be respected and to be shown that he is a real man—strong and special. A woman must tap into this in order to awaken a desire for the spiritual in him. And although it is called *Lo Lishma* (not for the sake of the Creator), one comes to *Lishma* (for the sake of the Creator) afterward.

Question:

And what if the man is really opposed to it? What should she do if her husband is actually hostile toward her involvement with Kabbalah?

Dr. Laitman:

Don't do anything! Leave him in this state and wait for him to come to it in accordance with the development of the *Reshimo* (recollection), possibly not even in this lifetime. However, a woman can be connected to the men's group on her own. There are many examples of that.

Even when we marry, we don't have to marry specifically those who are interested in the spiritual or those who are not, those who will study Kabbalah or those who will not. The most important thing when we plan to marry is that the future spouse knows that spiritual studies are a person's inner business. And if one of them decides that he wants to engage in spiritual development, the other is forbidden from interfering. She can help and join him, and they can walk together along this path like spiritual partners. But if not, they are forbidden from hindering this path for another person because this is an affair of the soul.

The Nature and Role of Women in Kabbalah

The Importance of Women in Kabbalah

"Kabbalah allots a woman the main role in the world. It is because the world's foremost development is its continuation, and it is a woman who continues generations. She extends this world from generation to generation; without her, it wouldn't be able to exist. Besides, since she forms the basis for the next generation's development—she educates and supports it—then naturally, progress and in general, life itself is impossible without a woman."

"...This stems from our roots because creation is of feminine gender. Malchut—a female component of the entire creation—is what, in fact, was created. And a man is only an auxiliary element that later perhaps leads her in some way, yet he exists for her sake. That is, men in this world assumed a totally wrong role. Their role in this world is auxiliary. Throughout the generations men are to help women continue and correctly develop offspring."

"...According to Kabbalah, the world exists around a woman. A so-called Malchut is a female component of the world. Zeir Anpin—her male part—exists only to help, support and fill her in accordance with her desires."

"...A female part in particular has to direct a male component how to act correctly for her sake. And then the world will move toward correction."

The Nature of Women and How It Differs from That of Men

"The essence of men and women is very different. As we know from Kabbalah, we represent two different worlds. The essence of a man comes from bestowal, and the essence of a woman—from reception. However, both of them certainly have a part of the other in them, and this is how we exist."

"...A woman is nature. It is a very strong force, and it is important for men to feel it. After all, it is not the same force that a man possesses. A man is more torn away from our nature. He is more of a philosopher and a rationalist. The force of a woman is much more real."

The Roles of Women and How They Differ from Those of Men

"There is no discrimination in spirituality. Women, like men, must attain adhesion with the Creator, the highest degree in creation. But women study differently from men, and so are the ways in which women can approach the Creator."

"...The only difference lies in the method. The beginning of the learning process is the same. That is why in our introductory courses there is no difference between the method provided for men and for women.

Later on, if a person goes deeper into the study of the actual Kabbalah, the difference in the method becomes apparent. Men and women begin to feel the world differently, because men and women are indeed two different worlds and have a different perception of creation."

Inner Work of a Woman

Seen Others as Corrected

Question:

In one of your talks you mentioned that women know how to love or have this ability and men don't. If we are all egoistic, then what kind of love can women give?

Dr's Answer:

Egoistic love. A woman can take care of the people whom she egoistically loves or respects.

Question:

Dear Rav, I have been studying Kabbalah for some time. I realize fully that I am totally egocentric and hope that the Creator will help me with this. But I also seem to note more than ever the egocentrism of other people in my everyday life, and I really don't like it. What can I do to overcome judgment and be at least polite to them if not compassionate, which I find very hard to do?

Dr's Answer:

What you are seeing in others is your own reflection, according to the rule, "All who fault, fault in their own flaw." However, if you loved them, then you would love their egoism as well - just like you would love your baby.

The Most Efficient Way to Aim toward the Goal

"By disseminating, you correct your 'self.' It seems like it's outside of you, in others, but in fact it's your spiritual body. So by bestowing and loving others, you're really bestowing and loving yourself! It's because this attitude to others allows you to acquire their desires and their Light."

"Try to find some kind of dissemination work to do; this will make you obligated and attached, and will motivate you to develop. The participation in the common work will increase your attainment, give you support, and enable you to correctly assess the value of this world."

Correction of a Woman's Soul

The Root of a Woman's Soul, and How Does It Differ From a Man's

"According to the wisdom of Kabbalah, the Creator, the giving force, is the spiritual root of the male part of reality, and the soul's desire to receive the abundance is the feminine root of the female part of reality."

"There are men and then there are women, because there is the Creator and then there's the creature, created by Him—two of them, two partners in this tango. There is the prototype of the Creator—the giving, dominant leader—that's the male root. And then there's the creature—receiving, drawing closer to the Creator, bringing them together—the female root.

The same applies to our life in this world. If we were to act correctly, clearly understanding how these two roots are implanted in nature and interconnected, we would do quite well—both men and women. After all, it is not just us, but all of Nature is divided from above downward into clear-cut male and female roots."

A Woman Is More Corrected and Closer to Nature than a Man

"A woman looks for the meaning of occurrences more than men do because she comes from the spiritual root where the feeling of need is deeper than in men. Therefore, she feels it more. A man comes from the side of the bestowing, from the side of the Creator, while a woman comes from the side of creation.

...All creation consists of ten *Sefirot*, separated into two parts: the first nine *Sefirot* pertain to the male structure, and the tenth

Sefira Malchut pertains to the female. To put it in simpler terms, *Sefirot* mean "properties." The first nine properties represent the property of bestowal, which comes from above in relation to *Malchut*, which is the creation. Hence, a man has an imprint of the first nine *Sefirot*, and a woman has an imprint of *Malchut*, the tenth *Sefira*. This tenth *Sefira* consists completely of the need to receive fulfillment."

"...However, in addition to the feeling of need, she also received a great power of opposition, restraint, and stability from Nature. Everything is in balance in a woman."

"A woman feels reality, the world, nature, and the ground underneath her feet, differently because according to her nature, she herself gives birth and continues life. There is a certain part in her that men do not have. After all, the Creator gives birth and continuation, and a woman gives birth and continuation. So, which one of us is more like the Creator is still in question. We, men, lack the force that would allow us to give birth and rear children. We are like a link between the Creator and the woman— just like Israel is the link between the Creator and the nations of the world."

A Woman's Greatest and Deepest Desire

"It expresses all the secrets of their hearts, all the depth of the desire for spiritual attainment and revelation of the answer to the question, "What is the meaning of my life?", which a woman asks, all the sorrow caused by the fact that she is incapable of attaining the spiritual alone and therefore feels a greater lack of power than a man, since she wants to reach her correction."

"...A woman is nature. It is a very strong force, and it is important for men to feel it. After all, it is not the same force that a man possesses. A man is more torn away from our nature. He is more of a philosopher and a rationalist. The force of a woman is much more real."

"...Her desire is natural and deep. Men can do anything they want and become confused in different things, while a woman is much more down-to-earth. She strives for the spiritual because she *wants* it. She understands that there is no life without it. Men can still be tempted to go in different directions, but a woman's desire is much more deep, natural, and genuine."

Question:

If a female soul is the will to receive, how will this change during correction?

Answer:

"A woman is the desire, and a man is the correction of the desire, the intention of bestowal. In our world, a woman waits for a man to do something, such as to marry her, and her part in this is relatively passive.

This comes from the spiritual roots: When the soul acquires the intention of bestowal, it is called a man, whereas a soul that's unable to bestow is called a woman. The parts of the *Kli* or soul are also called male and female for the same reason.

So, regardless of your gender in this world, start to actively participate in your personal correction and humanity's collective correction!"

Women Crossing the Machsom

"A woman enters Kabbalah and the Upper World in the same way a man does."

"...During the period of incarnation when we are located in our world, before we pass the *Machsom* (the boundary separating our world from the spiritual one) and leave the perceptions of our world, what type of body (male or female) our soul inhabits is significant. Afterward, when souls pass the *Machsom* and enter the perceptions of the Upper World, it is no longer significant who is a man and who is a woman. We will all be Kabbalists - the soul does not have a gender. Of course, there are differences between souls, but they are not purely based on gender. The differences regard what part of the common soul each of the souls relates to."

"A man needs the desire for spiritual advancement that a woman must give him. She must support and encourage him, and give him strength. She should expect that he will attain the spiritual. Due to this, equipped with strength and armor, a man sets out for spiritual attainments the same way that, formerly, he left his cave to hunt and bring home food.

This is a very important part, through which a woman supplements the work of a man, and without it a man cannot reach the spiritual. Women are able to do this work wonderfully. If we talk to psychologists, we see that everything a man does in the world, he does in order to be liked by women. Pride, strength, power, and the desire to rise above others, are to a great extent roused by a man's need to appear a man in the eyes of a woman. This is a reflection of a spiritual state, which, of course, is not connected to our egoism, but the attitude itself remains.

In other words, an unsatisfied desire that emanates from a woman, reaches a man, and the man uses this desire in order to reach the spiritual. We can say that a woman wakes the desire in a man, and the man turns this desire to the Upper Force, acquires spiritual advancement for himself, and shares it with the woman."

How a Woman Knows She Is Advancing Sufficiently and Correctly

"Only the Creator knows and only He can give the answer regarding our advancement. We must turn to Him with this request and demand an answer. In Kabbalah it is called going "above reason," meaning above our knowledge and understanding. Every step we make, if it is genuine, should make us rise to the next degree. But the thoughts and desires in the next degree are not just opposite to the ones in the current degree; they are completely different!"

The Ways to Approach the Creator

Question:

We received a question concerning women's intention.
When a woman does dissemination or reads, should her appeal be directed at the Creator, or should she address the Creator through the male part?

Dr's Answer:

No, her appeal should be to the Creator directly. Women pray the same way as men do. Only the need for fulfillment, which should be realized while she does this, goes through the male part.

Let's suppose that there is a woman who is somewhere on the edge of the earth, and she has no men who study Kabbalah nearby. She studies with us through the Internet in a different language. How it happens is completely irrelevant.

Still, if a woman prays and asks the Upper Force for spiritual elevation, it will nonetheless come through the *Kli*, which is called the male part, and which is ultimately the common soul, from which she receives the fulfillment.

Question:

So, she needs to appeal directly to the Creator to the extent that she feels Him?

Dr's Answer:

We learn that in almost all cases, it is carried out through the inclusion of *Malchut* into the *Tet Rishonot* (the first nine *Sefirot*). This means that the female part tunes into the male part, and then into the Creator.

...It is simply the way this process is arranged. First Adam was created, and then from Adam, Chava and everyone else (their children and so on) were created. It happens the same way with us. We raise our pleas about fulfillment by following the same path. In other words, Chava (the female part) should transmit it to Adam, and he, in turn, transmits it above.

Can a Woman's Soul Reincarnate in the Body of a Man, or Vice Versa?

"The soul does have a specific gender: male or female. That attribute extends from the root of creation, from the very beginning. *Zeir Anpin* (male) and *Malchut* (female) of the world of *Atzilut* are the prototypes of the genders in our world, and there are no greater opposites than these.

Throughout the system of creation, built from up downward, there is a division, a separation into a feminine part and masculine part.

The lower the degree of creation, the coarser and simpler it becomes, and the more overlap there is between the masculine and feminine parts.

For example, in plants there is almost no division by sex. But the more the creatures develop, meaning the higher up they are on the ladder of evolution, the more distinct they become.

In the spiritual world, this oppositeness is very obvious. One does not cancel the other, but complements it. Without the feminine part, the system of creation is inconceivable. The masculine part depends on the feminine part and waits for it."

"Yes, it is true men and women have different kinds of souls. But the souls of men are neither better nor worse than those of women. They are simply different kinds of souls, and hence their corrections are different."

The Women's Desire as the Engine of Creation

Question:

What does it mean to strengthen the collective desire of the women? How can I add my own desire to it?

Answer:

In the science of Kabbalah, we study that the entire universe consists of two parts: the Light and the vessel, desire. The desire is considered feminine, and its means of fulfillment is considered masculine. This is why it is most important to strengthen the women's desire. Virtually everything develops through it—the upper one and the lower one.

Even in our world we know that if it weren't for women and their desires, the world would cease to exist a long time ago. A woman compels a man, forces him to work, obtain income, and build a home. She runs the household: She maintains, gives birth, and nurtures.

Thus, according to nature, a man is the provider of energy, force, and a woman is the force that creates everything, brings up the children, educates, and cares for them. No matter what a man does, by definition and even without being aware of it, he does it because of women who awaken these desires in him. The minus, the female part, always causes the action of the plus, the male part.

Everything in nature is arranged in this manner: animals, plants, and, naturally, us. Maybe we are unable to feel it because of our egoistic properties; we run away from it, obscure it. However, in reality the female part is always the foundation, the main determinant of our movement forward. The man subconsciously asks himself whether he will get approval in the woman's eyes as a result of his actions.

It is truly like this; this is nature.

Thus, women should take upon themselves the responsibility for directing, encouraging, and readjusting men correctly, as a mother of young children. To the extent that women assume this responsibility and support the men, the men will behave differently, study, communicate with each other, and exert themselves.

We need to radically, categorically break away from what is going on in our world because it is all upside-down. We need to make the women's part decisive, meaning to feel the women's need for achieving the goal, while the men's part has to be responsible for filling this need, this desire for fulfillment.

A Convention That Will Ignite the Flame in Our Hearts

There is an upcoming convention, and our entire world group needs this special awakening on the part of the women. I am very happy that the women are enthusiastic over this special event. They are ready to do whatever they can, and I hope it will bear fruit.

We expect this convention to be a great ascent that will provide all of us with a new deficiency. In every family, the woman "fires up" her husband, and we want this flare to be a million times more powerful, and that a real burning desire aimed at the goal will surround us. The women are ready and able to do that.

On the whole, a purposeful woman is more than 90% of the success. It is with good reason that we say that behind every successful man there is a woman. It is also true in spirituality. I can hardly imagine a man's success along the spiritual path without female support. So, why do we need all these hardships if we can connect according to the law of root and branch? It is written, "A man and a woman—Divinity between them." The connection begins in the family, continues in the group, and reaches the connection with the Creator. So, eventually, we will resemble Him as one image of one man.

Wake Up the Men!

Question:
How should women support the unification among the men?

Answer:
This is a very powerful and important action from the women's end. They can motivate the men to advance spiritually: to unite, study, and disseminate.

In the same way, in the spiritual world, *Zeir Anpin* starts moving and acting only when *Malchut*, the female part, motivates him to do so by raising *MAN* to him and demanding correction.

A man will not awaken without a woman and her desire—both at home and in the group. Therefore, the female part has to wake up and awaken the male part because otherwise the men won't attain the goal.

We turn to all the women of the world *Kli*, asking them to unite together and put pressure on the men in different ways. Then the men will feel that they have to advance and that they cannot calm down.

Woman Is Where Changes Take Place

To influence the men in a wholesome and powerful way, the women must also unite, but they should unite with an understanding of the principles of our work and what exactly to demand from the men. To do so, they must know what the Light is that the men need to draw and what it has to beget.

A woman in spirituality is a force even greater than a man. A man is just a force, a screen, whereas a woman is the place where all kinds of changes occur. She begets a new rung and nourishes it. Conception, nurturing, and maturing to adulthood, all of it lies within the female's part of the collective or individual soul.

As regards a man, he only delivers the Light. It is said that he "provides the whitening," and that completes his role, as it were. After that, he resides within a mother and through her provides the forces to develop the souls.

As regards the offspring, everything comes from the mother, the female part. All spiritual growth goes through a woman, and it is the female part that begets souls. The same is mentioned in the Torah. For example, "Abraham" and "Sarah" are two parts of the soul who beget a new soul, and their more advanced state is regarded as "Isaac." Who gives birth to him? Obviously, it is Sarah.

We must function as nature dictates. Having aligned ourselves with the material nature, we will move on from it to the spiritual one, thanks to which we will accomplish what we set out to do without harming ourselves.

On the contrary, the more harm we inflict by indulging our egoism, the more we will scream about the "equality" that in reality ruins families and society, and the fewer our chances will become. Some politicians may benefit from it, but it won't be us.

Be More Insolent With the Creator

Question:

We have been talking about the fact that we have to ask for everything only from the Creator. But what should I do if I am shy? Or maybe I am not even worthy of asking Him for anything?

Answer:

I would advise you not to ask, but to *demand*. If we are ashamed to ask the Creator, it means we feel that we are still distant from Him, that we don't have anything in common with Him.

Men often feel proud at first and behave like little roosters: "Why would I ask Him for anything? What should I ask Him for?" So on one hand, there is shame, and on the other - pride. Yet, both of these sensations will gradually pass. If a person becomes included in the group, it happens very quickly.

I would advise you to be more insolent. The Creator likes it when a person says, "I deserve this. You have to help me!"

Unify to Give Birth to the Creator

The creature descends from the perfection of the <u>world of Infinity</u> into our world and, before reaching it, begins to divide into two parts: male and female. These two parts, which previously existed in total harmony, try to preserve their mutual connection. But at the last moment, when their connection breaks, they split into two. It triggers the creation of the system of the impure worlds that distanced the male part from the female one.

As they were infinitely unified in the world of Infinity, they became infinitely withdrawn from each other in the impure worlds. That is where they fell into our world from, the world where the male and female parts are fully separated from each

43

other and exist at a minimal degree of connection, in order to sustain the existence in the still, vegetative, and animate forms of matter, as well as at the "speaking" level. The force of connection manifests in them not as cooperation and reciprocity but as their consumption of each other. Hence, their state is totally opposite to the spiritual world.

The wisdom of Kabbalah states that our world came into existence with the creation of the perfect creature, Adam, that divided into two parts. They separated and severed the contact with one another, yet still preserved some connection and interdependence. This begot the life in our world, the life full of suffering.

Being disconnected from the spiritual world, we have to come to the realization that only our internal, spiritual unification will create a place for the revelation of the Creator. And then it will be called: "Husband and wife, and the *Shechina* between them."

The unification and mutual inclusion of multiple male and female parts complimenting each other will result in the revelation of the Creator within them, which is their mutual, perfect part where the Upper Light unfolds.

Help Me Cope With Men!

Question from women:

Why have you decided to organize a women's convention for the first time in history? How have we deserved it?

Answer:

This is due to the fact that above all we men need your support and your pressure. It's not the first time I've talked about this, but now we all miss it very much: both men and women. As the head of the world group, I am very interested in a serious women's group that will unite and give men overall strength, a common desire that will be organized correctly and put pressure on them. It's very important to me. Help me cope with men!

Question:

What should be the result of the women's convention? In what state should men be after it?

Answer:

After the women's convention, men should feel that they are obliged to carry out the women's will. We learn this in Kabbalah. Women's desires/*Aviut* rise to the men's desires, and the men realize them. That is how things work in nature.

Unity

A Letter to the Beloved in the Front

Question:

How can we connect what we study in TES about Malchut that raises MAN to Zeir Anpin, the prayer from which the spiritual birth begins, to the women's convention?

Answer:

True, it all begins from the female deficiency; this is the real deficiency, the deficiency of Malchut. Zeir Anpin symbolizes the male, and Malchut, Nukva, symbolizes the woman.

We are expecting a strong general desire to be accumulated and gathered in the women in this connection above all differences and individualism. We hope that the women will help one another to connect and will be able to raise their general deficiency so high that it will be felt in the spiritual system.

If it is felt and revealed in the general system, then we men will also feel it. I asked the women to write a letter with a request, a demand, an appeal from the women's convention to the men's convention but, in fact, in the spiritual world it doesn't really matter whether this request is expressed in writing. The main thing is that it will be incorporated in the system of the general desire of creation, of the general reality.

A letter, however, can hasten this bestowal and bring it together, since it does obligate us to respond. Let's hope that we will receive a very strong push from the women's convention, a stimulation and demand to draw the Light that Reforms.

If we try to attain the Light according to the women's request, we will have a form that is closer to bestowal compared to the form we could create on our own. Women can even ask egoistically for help for themselves to connect and attain spirituality. But when this desire is aimed at bestowal and connection, at least a little, it is connected to the wisdom of Kabbalah, and incorporated in a man. He, in turn, accepts it as a spiritual desire, since it is already a foreign demand. So by fulfilling this demand, we create a much stronger spiritual act than if we tried to create it by ourselves, for ourselves.

Don't Wait, Act!

Question:
When men unite, they cause a feeling of incomparable thrill in women. We women are looking very much forward to this.

Answer:
You should not wait for this. You need to act. Otherwise, nothing will happen. You should pressure men, help them, that is, behave like a wife at home in relation to her husband. That is how the entire women's part of the world group must affect the men's part. In principle, the soul is composed of male and female parts, and the Creator is between them.

You should not rely on men only. On their own, they would not have built the world. They cannot give birth, raise children, or perform household duties. That is why they need support, help, direction, and pressure. This is what a woman usually does at home, helping her husband.

The entire *Kli* (vessel) is the women's part, not the men's. The men do attract the Light, but to the women's desire, to the women's aspiration. Thus, it is necessary to match the women's and men's parts correctly. However, don't wait! On the contrary, if you do not cause an urgent need to attract the Light in men, they will not do that. This is how we are organized.

The Women's Group Is Beyond Hierarchies

Question:

Due to recent changes (from the women's convention), a big importance of women's unity has emerged. There are women who are more active and less active in our group. For the active women, we organize certain activities and separate workshops, thereby creating a few circles in the women's community.

As a result, there are many unhappy women who think that we have split this community. Is it right to do this in the women's group?

Answer:

I believe it is incorrect. The mass should be as uniform as possible. I do not divide anyone. Some women participate less, no matter for what reason, some more. I never look for reasons, especially if we are talking about women, not men. Men can be pressed, but women should not be, and in general, women should be treated as equal to men. But they must not make any divisions between themselves. Absolutely not!

Question:

So, on what principle could the women's group be formed?

Answer: According to the principle of the circle, everyone is equal. If I want to advance towards spirituality, I do not need earthly levels: What honors I would be rewarded, or how many stars they would attach to me. What is important for me is spiritual ascent, and I do not ask anything for myself. If it is possible to invest my efforts, I invest them. If there is no opportunity, then there is none. But a person should wait for the highest reward for his invested efforts, rather than have power and position in the group. What for? This is incorrect!

There are people who have organizational skills; it is another matter. We appoint them to be responsible for this or that because we benefit if they are engaged in these duties or something else, but in any case, we should not divide the group.

We have people who work very hard for the group. So what? Are they supposed to get more? For what reason?

Women's Work along Two Lines

Question:

Our virtual women's group of ten gathers after every lecture. We share our impressions, read Shamati together, and there is a feeling that we recharge one another. Is there anything spiritual in that or are women exempt from doing that?

Answer:

First of all, women need everything that men need. Second, a person is where his thoughts are, so you are doing a great job. Connect and think that it's very important.

If you are not connected, you will not be able to influence the men. Each woman is powerless by herself. Only if you are connected, at least in a group of ten, will you be able to influence the men.

They will begin to subconsciously feel that you are pressuring them, that you demand of them just like a wife demands of her husband.

This is how we are made! And it's very important! So encouraging and demanding at the same time is a woman's work along two lines. We have to use that. Men who don't perceive that will deprive themselves of the strongest means to advance! They mustn't refuse that, or they will have no incentive.

It's the female nature that can obligate a man to act. Even psychologists and historians speak about the fact that a man can do anything for a woman. Such mutual cooperation is part of our nature.

So you have to act together and to influence the men's group together and actually demand that they pay attention to you and take your yearning seriously. It is serious work. I see that wherever there is a strong women's group, the men are also successful.

Convergence of Two Desires

Question:

How can I correctly prepare for the women's convention?

Answer:

First, we should review the materials that relate to women's work.

Basically, in our time, there is not much difference between men's and women's work because a gradual convergence is taking place. We see how the women of the world occupy leadership positions, are heads of state, ministers, and managers of various companies. Today, they are equally involved with men in all the spheres of activity.

Although women are inherently more inclined to something specific, standard, stable, and not the activities that constantly demand drastic changes, the time has come when both desires— male and female—come together in our world and in the spiritual world. This occurs in accordance with the spiritual roots, and thus it is necessary to think how to bring them together even closer. This is what we are going to be engaged in at the convention: The women must understand the <u>goal</u> before them.

Never before have women become united together. We had all sorts of attempts to unite in groups, during general conventions, but there wasn't such a convention to make the desire of all the women as one woman's desire, to create a unified image of women's desire.

That is why the preparation for the convention is to think more about it, read, clarify the questions on this topic, and upload all the questions and answers on the website.

The most important thing is to be in a good mood, good spirit. Those who come here will inevitably enter this atmosphere. Those who will be connected to us should be prepared to get into it: They should be free of all their activities and feel as though they are here with us. I think we will give them the feeling of complete presence at the convention.

Women's Questions in Preparation for the Convention

Question:

How can women create a strong common desire to maximize the ability to support the men during the convention?

Answer:

Women are doing spiritual work just as men do. The only difference is that the style of their interconnection is somewhat different from the connection between the men.

With men, it all starts with a very simple friendship, with shared activities. They swim together, sit around, share meals and study. With women, this connection is much more complicated. But when they set a higher goal for themselves and understand that for the sake of this goal they need to unite, they can accomplish it and achieve the goal. That is, the exalted goal becomes like a master for them, and they're prepared to unite for its sake.

Question:

Do women need to prepare for the convention in some special way? Perhaps we should do it together somehow or correspond with each other? Or should we only unite internally?

Answer:

The importance of unification should be the same in women as in men. Also, they need to understand that they need to achieve unity. Women are able to unite for the sake of a higher goal, and they need to explore and scrutinize this possibility.

The Bible tells about how Moses' sister, Miriam, united all the women together before exiting Egypt, how the women worked on themselves in Egypt, and how it was precisely that feminine part which nurtured Moses, that is, the force that then pulls us out of Egypt.

Question:

What should women expect from the workshops?

Answer:

The women, like the men, need to discuss all the details of unification. Let them try to do that; let them discover what is for them and what isn't. In this manner, they will find their own path in a practical way, since otherwise it won't work.

On one hand, women ask, "Why not?" But when you offer them the work of unification, they say, "This isn't for us!" And so a problem arises. And it's unclear what can be done, what action to take, and how to approach this problem.

Women need to unite for a common cause, like in a huge number of existing women's organizations, where women can unite in order to achieve something **not between, but outside of themselves**. So let them unite in order to achieve something outside themselves as well, and for that purpose they can connect, not against anyone, but for the sake of accomplishing something. They can do it!

Question:

Do women need to unite in order to achieve the goal or in order for the men to reach it?

Answer:

They need to unite to attain the result together. Let them clarify this, and they will see the middle point into which they need to fit exactly to complement the men. And in no way is their work any less than the work of men; it's actually greater.

Question:

How should a woman prepare her husband for the convention?

Answer:

You wash, dress, and feed him, then hand him his backpack, and let him go to school. I'm speaking absolutely seriously: Prepare him like you would a child. That is, let him know that you expect great accomplishments from him, that you hope that throughout the convention he'll really go in the right direction with good and necessary thoughts. That's how you get him ready. When it comes to that, a woman has what's called the wisdom of life.

Question:

How do men work correctly with women's support during the workshops?

Answer:

Men shouldn't pay attention to it yet. Later, when we really become properly interconnected, we'll feel the women's influence, pressure on us.

It's good when we can sense that; it obliges us. Let's hope that we'll be able to feel that, too.

Women Will Succeed!

Question:

Women often find it difficult to act together with each other. How can we force ourselves to support our girlfriends, take care of the women's group, and participate in the general women's events when the very thought of connecting with each other is unbearable?

Answer:

This is only at the beginning, especially for women because they are not used to connecting with each other. Every woman is on her own; she does not need to connect with others as long as she has a connection with a man.

But spiritual ascent requires a connection between women and their joint effect on the men. That is why the ultimate goal is to have them begin to unite; afterward they will start to feel that it is possible to be together and unite.

The Women's Convention: Rising Above the Imaginary Show

Question:

What should be the intention of the women during the convention?

Answer:

First of all, during the time of the convention, we will direct our thoughts. For this we must hold the correct preparation workshops and discussions, which are devoted to our connection and unity.

All of the convention is directed towards this, in order to be a general, complete "one," leaving below all the desires and thoughts, our daily egoistic intentions, everything that concerns this world. Each one needs to take from within her heart her point and connect it with the others. Imagine that in front of you there is a basket or plate, and we throw all of our points in the heart there and connect them. Then within them, in their connection, we will feel the Upper World.

This needs to be the intention, to rise above ourselves, to forget everything that is happening at home, all the problems, all the daily circumstances of this world, to understand that it happens in order for us to rise above all of it.

The entire world exists so that we will understand that we need to transfer ourselves to the side of the Creator. Outside of ourselves, we discover the real world. Then it will be clear that this world was made like an intention aimed at me, like a special theatrical performance where I need to be until I understand that all of this is only a show that it is like a dream from which I need to wake up and begin to develop outside of it. There I will find my real self in an eternal and complete state. It is to this state that we must enter.

And our world doesn't get lost; it will always continue with its theatrical show, but I will already understand the reason why each time I am given a new action. And each time I will rise above this action, higher and higher, in a denser and denser manner with the other things, until I finish all the work in this world, until the general unity above it is in complete connection. And that will be our *Gmar Tikkun* (the final correction)—one, united spiritual woman.

Actions on the Home Front Prepare the Weapon for the Attack in the Desert

Question:

The Creator is providing the perfect conditions lately for us to express our good attitude towards Him in the two coming conventions: the women's convention, One Global Woman, and the men's convention, A Flame in the Desert. How should we prepare in order to successfully fulfill the opportunity we were given?

Answer:

It is very important to respect the women's convention and not look down on it. This is because it is a spiritual action and not a corporeal one. It is a very meaningful action in spirituality, which is no less important than the men's convention. I see them as totally equal, and I really hope that the general deficiency that the women will attain and stabilize in this convention will influence us and strongly operate on us, the men. We will reach the convention in the desert ready and equipped with this great, good, and correct deficiency with yearning for connection, and we will be able to reveal and put together the first part of the corrected soul from all these parts.

Every person has his weak and strong points. But spirituality is a perfect system, and so everyone making a revelation fills all the others. We fill one another mutually. I hope that this will really be realized. If we take serious steps towards connection, we will succeed.

The first part of the corrected soul is the goal of the two coming conventions in order to reach the revelation of the Creator to the created being, in order to bring Him contentment, to reveal the first level of the 125 spiritual levels.

The Unified Women's Desire

Question:

Why is the upcoming women's convention called "One Global Woman"? What does "global woman" mean?

Answer:

There is only one soul in the world, a unified desire that was split into two complementary parts: male and female. They, in turn, were broken into a huge number of individual desires.

Our job is to gather the female and male parts together. At the same time, they rise above their routine earthly desires, correcting the desire to receive to the desire to bestow, and then two desires emerge that, on the one hand, are opposite, but on the other hand, are spiritual. And then both parts begin to connect with each other into one unified, common creation that is called Adam. In principle, this is what we have to do.

Men will gather at their convention a week after the women's convention. And before that, we will discuss with the women how it is possible to unite into one unified women's desire. I hope that we will succeed. At least, this is very important for the men and for all of us. We have never done this before, and now the time has come.

I never do anything in advance. When there is a need to realize the next state, I talk about this and then we begin to think about how to implement it. Now we have come to the state when we really need to get together and try to unite into a single woman's desire.

I congratulate all the women in the world with our great internal holiday. We will try to make it important, light, serious, and at the same time fun!

The Ideal Women's Unity

Question:

What is women's unity? What is its ideal form?

Answer:

The ideal form of women's unity is that you will feel not yourself but everyone as one unified woman, a single image, a single desire. This desire will be above your body and your individual calculations, above various misunderstandings and mutual rejection.

When for the sake of the goal you are able to rise above yourself and create the image of a unified woman, it will be ideal because it will be based on disregard for egoism.

Begin to rise a bit above your current egoism, above all sorts of minor problems, petty earthly nonsense, and even if it's not yet an ideal woman, you will get an ideal little girl.

Then, egoism will grow, women's troublesome problems will emerge, and you will rise above them, becoming aware that all this is given to you on purpose to create the image of a more mature ideal woman. Do not think that it will be easy. The entire work is based on this: to unite above all possible rejections.

To Break through the Cocoon and Enter the Spiritual World

Question:

What kind of inner preparation needs to be done prior to the Women's Convention?

Answer:

In order to break the barrier between us, to somehow soften the situation, we need to hold a workshop with the group or some kind of event, in order to feel that to some extent it is possible to facilitate the trend towards building a relationship: not to sit distanced from each other and delve within yourself, but to exit yourself, somewhat rise above yourself, outward toward the others, and then we will find our spiritual vessel, *Kli.*

It is a clear female emotion when I am inside myself, "I within myself." With the men it doesn't stand out so much. On the one hand, women overcome this with more difficulty, and on the other hand, more easily, since it is easier for them to determine where this "cocoon" is within them. A woman feels very clearly that it is "I within myself," whereas a man doesn't. Until a man reaches this "cocoon," a lot of time has to pass.

Thus, I suggest for women to hold several meetings, discussions on this subject. It could be a workshop. I think it will be enough to at least begin to exit ourselves. And afterward, during the convention, we will talk about it and deal with it.

Question:

What would you advise women who understand the importance of their presence at the convention, but prefer not to physically go there? How is it possible to help them overcome this "cocoon"?

Answer:

I think one simply needs to decide and to work on yourself without paying attention to those around you: "We must do this now!" and begin to operate, constantly trying to break through the shell of isolation. You will see how much, on one hand, it is difficult, but on the other hand, the constant blows from within from this "cocoon" will break it in the end. But inevitably one must do it! Without that, we won't feel that we are in the spiritual world that is found outside us, beyond the boundary of this "cocoon."

Family Relationships

...All of this is created for a reason. Relatives and close ones—aunts, uncles, grandmas, grandpas, and so on—did not appear in nature without a reason. All of this comes from a special particular hierarchy of spiritual forces, which descend on us.

In accordance with this, such relationships are based on causes and consequences that result in our world, as well, but we establish them incorrectly. The fact that we have grandparents, parents, sons and daughters, and so on—all of that is correct; however, the relationships between them are established incorrectly. In any case, the presence of all of these levels, and also a need for interaction between us, come from nature...

...This is why you are given a family with all of its problems.

Run away from these problems into the Upper Worlds, and you will find completely new states there, rather than a medicine for the various insignificant corporeal concerns. This is precisely why everything is created. This is why when I tell you, "You have no way out, you need to open up a book!" you object, "Why do I need to read a book in order to solve a corporeal problem?" No, the corporeal problem is not solved here, since it is given to you only in order to push you out into a higher world.

[A grandparent asks]:

Can I give a Kabbalistic education to my grandchildren?

Dr. Laitman:

...I am allowed to bring it [Kabbalistic education] only to my kids, because the parents determine this; it is from the order of nature. They determine what they want to make out of their kids – to give them this or that education, but not to the grandchildren. The grandchildren, my grandchildren, have an owner, namely my son or my daughter, and they determine it, not me. I can advise or ask or maybe influence them, but not to determine. I'm not allowed from the standpoint of nature.

Balancing Home, the Outside World, and Kabbalah

Question:
Do Kabbalists live ordinary lives?

Dr. Laitman:

The wisdom of Kabbalah necessitates that every person take an active part in this world: work, raise a family, learn and teach. In addition to the normal routine, one must also attain the purpose of Creation – a spiritual contact with the Creator. The Creator created this world and everything in it precisely as it is to assist us in learning how to reach His spiritual degree on the existing reality. That is why the wisdom of Kabbalah does not rely on fasting, abstention, or deprivation of any sort. There is no coercion and no punishments in this world or in the next.

...We must only labor as much as we can. It is not as if we are demanded to do something that is beyond our abilities. Let us say that we need 6-7 hours of sleep a day. We work about 8 hours, waste about two hours getting back and forth from work, eat, bathe, and give time to our families.

This is not what Kabbalah requires from us. Kabbalah requires the time that remains after all the necessary occupations have been carried out. If we invest all our free time in Kabbalah, that will certainly be enough.

Everything Requires a Skill

Question:

How can a working woman with children combine preparation for the convention with daily domestic chores?

Answer:

I advise her to listen to our programs while doing domestic chores; she can do so by turning on our television channel or Internet site. For a woman, it is easier to accomplish. She can switch on the TV and continue working around the house. This alone puts a person under the influence of the right environment.

In addition, if you can, read my blog daily. As much as the time allows, enter the *Sviva Tova* (Good Environment—the worldwide Internet connection) site and answer the questions. Usually, a woman's time is more limited than a man's, but if she finds the time for all of this, then she should try listening to Kabbalistic music.

If a person is eager but can't find time to do more, then such conditions are arranged for him or her from Above, and it is enough for preparation. And the rest we will do together at the convention.

The most important thing about studying is to dedicate two or three hours in the morning to these endeavors before going to work. We take that time only from ourselves. These 2-3 hours are enough. It is important to learn with the right intention; ask ourselves why we do it. Aim is the single most important thing!

...It is imperative that we understand the separation between our obligations to the society we live in and to our personal spiritual growth. Knowing where to draw the line and how to contribute to both will free us from much confusion and misconceptions about spirituality.

The rule in life should be simple and straightforward: In everyday life we obey the rule of law; in spiritual life we're free to evolve individually. It turns out that individual freedom can only be achieved through our choice in spiritual evolvement, where others must not interfere.

...In accordance to this spiritual point that has emerged in him, a person begins to aspire towards other objects and therefore completely alters his friends, connections and hobbies. This occurs to such a degree that he does not even find anything to talk about with people who are close to him because all his aspirations are towards something they lack.

People don't understand that life is meaningless if it's not used to attain the goal that has been set before every person. The sky, the earth, and every one of us were created for attaining this goal, and not for creating a marriage on the animate level and becoming a slave of your partner's egoism. So the conclusion to be made from this is: In all life situations, your behavior should be determined only by the spiritual goal!

Children

Teaching Children Kabbalah

...Children need to be taken into account from childhood, during a time when they take everything from us, since a child is educated through examples of the behavior patterns that he sees from his parents and then from the broader surroundings. If we know how to give the children the correct way to behave from the very beginning, from the age of zero, (and this also means that the parents themselves have to be educated), together with the ego that grows in them from year to year, then we would be able to give them the means to correct themselves above the ego, progressing more and more. That is actually called "the education."

Education is to give the child a means to be above his nature, to control his nature. We are already lost since they educated us incorrectly, and now we have to correct ourselves. We will be the first generation to correct ourselves. But after us, we must attempt for the following generation to already be corrected. From very early on, our children will absorb everything and know the solution to all the problems and sorrows of this world and how to go above them and attain, not only through detachment from the problems we have here but by reaching an eternal, complete, and happy life now, abounding in all fulfillments.

[A mother asks]:

"How do I tell my 6-year-old daughter about the spiritual world? I have already told her about the ego and the will to bestow, to love. That is, after she herself told me, "I have a dot of Light in my heart."

Dr. Laitman:

How to tell her about the spiritual world? Very simply that there is something above us which rules over us, and from Him, forces descend upon us and direct us. And why do those forces work upon us?

In order to awaken in us the will to ascend back to that high level, the eternal, good and beautiful. It is the level in which we love each other, where we connect to each other, where we are as one man in one heart.

This state is called the spiritual world, the Upper World. When you explain it to your child in this way, it is all true. Never lie to kids, but explain it to them a little bit - the truth.

The basic principle of the right education is actually very simple: Parents should not tell a child what to do, but only *how* to do it, if the child asks.

And what happens until then? Parents should use their ingenuity to find alternative ways to awaken in a child the desire to do what needs to be done. This way, the desire for it will be the child's own. This is the right education.

Parents who pressure their children, who try to forcefully teach them certain information or habits, raise a broken generation.

The wisdom of Kabbalah, on the other hand, is against any kind of violence or pressure. "There is no coercion in spirituality." No coercion means that everything exists and is done only out of one's own will. What parents have to do is to awaken that will.

Question:

How can we educate children today, when they are surrounded by so many temptations? How can we help them avoid the influence of the environment on their small egos, and give them an education that will make spiritual development become the most important thing in their lives?

Dr. Laitman:

This is much easier than it seems. If we give children the right examples, then they will copy them onto their relatively pure matter. It's written that educating a child is like writing on a clean sheet of paper, since he is still not damaged by all the social "garbage," confusion and egoistical calculations, as is the case with adults.

Obviously, children are also egoists; they want to deceive one another in order to succeed. They make calculations very quickly and act for the sake of self-interest. But their behavior is natural, and therefore appears different than ours. With the same natural ease, they absorb our explanations about the system they exist in, about the world and the correct kind of relationships.

Such explanations penetrate deep into their feelings, and thus you are able to build their inner system.

It can be compared to a computer system. By itself, the PC is nothing but a piece of metal that is incapable of doing anything. But when you install a program into it, the program determines how all of the computer's components will connect and how they will function. If you install another program into the computer, then it will cancel the previous one and instruct the components to connect differently. In the same way, when you install a new program into the child's "hardware," he will live according to the program's instructions. This is called "raising a human being," and the outcome depends on the spiritual level of the adults that are raising the child.

Dr. Laitman:

...Everyone should correct not his character, but how he uses it...

...The wisdom of Kabbalah states: "Teach the boy according to the boy's way." "His way" means only to direct him, to give him love, bestowal and giving, so that he will express himself in the right direction of bestowal to others, using all his personality traits and everything he has naturally. But *he* should express it, express himself. Here we must not limit him. We must not interfere; "there is no compulsion in spirituality"...

...If a person is born with a certain set of personality traits and predispositions, don't try to change that. Just explain to him how he can fulfill them correctly, in the best outstanding way.

Question:

So with the people of the future, in relation to their children, will there be punishment? Are you saying that punishment is not a correction?

Dr. Laitman:

There is punishment, but punishment should be such that a person understands that this is the punishment that comes from nature against his behavior because it is not in balance with nature.

...It is just like when one stands across from a fire or on the edge of a cliff; he knows that he shouldn't be doing it. Why? It's because that is the law. There is nothing to ask. He can do all kinds of things but the law is clearly in front of him. If he jumps off the cliff or goes into the fire, that's it, his life is finished. This is the way a person should see it. He should see how things are bad for him because he went against the law of nature.

Question:

From your perspective, how does this mechanism work? What causes the change in the child if I begin to explain to him about the influence of the society on a person, about the desire to receive, not to go deeply into it? One hears about the soul of Adam ha Rishon to which we are all connected and that all the power and the entire law of reality operates there, i.e., the connection between souls as one soul, that one Light fills them, and that this is called Ein Sof. There, the creation and the Creator are connected together in eternal adhesion.

Dr. Laitman:

If one hears something like this, similar to this, then he is influenced without his knowing it, without his awareness, by an Upper, special, power from there called "the Surrounding Light" or "the Light that Reforms." Whether he wants it or not, he becomes similar by the simplest game that he is not aware of; that doesn't matter. However, because of this, he changes. I use this system in all kinds of things.

What does Baal HaSulam say? Put him into a society. It doesn't matter if he wants it, just as long as he says he is ready to participate in something. Gradually, he will be among other people who will influence him. He will want to be liked by the society. He will need to perform some activities. Suddenly, he will feel that it is worthwhile for him to participate on behalf of the society and, thus, he will continue with it. He will continue with it in order to get prizes, rewards, etc. from the society.

Then, he will begin to feel what is called "grace from Above" that in and of itself is a good thing even if he doesn't get medals or prizes. He even will be embarrassed that he received a medal once he sees how great it is. No one even recognizes its greatness. He now knows the *Gadlut* (adultness) of bestowal. It suddenly comes to him to such an extent that he doesn't want anyone to even know about it. It is that precious to him. This is called "grace from Above."

Where does this "beast" get this? It happens because he carried out activities that were compatible to *Ein Sof*, to *Adam ha Rishon*, and he didn't even know about it, but that's how it works. After all, he is within a system.

The Role of Women in Nurturing Their Children with Respect to Kabbalah

"It is written that we should "educate the youth according to his way." This means that not only parents but a child as well should clearly see where he is going, and he should want it. Then he will accept education, he will demand it.

...Parents who pressure their children, who try to forcefully teach them certain information or habits, raise a broken generation.

...The wisdom of Kabbalah, on the other hand, is against any kind of violence or pressure. 'There is no coercion in spirituality.' No coercion means that everything exists and is done only out of one's own will. What parents have to do is to awaken that will.

...Our problem is that no one is doing that, and the whole education system is flawed. Hence, our task is to help parents understand this principle of Kabbalists—everything stems from a person's free will, and all we have to do is to help its free development."

"Knowledge of the laws operating in our roots and of how the Upper Forces operate, gives us an absolutely precise understanding of how to ideally and most correctly treat and raise a child, how to interact with a fetus and a newborn, as well as with a teenager and adolescent. It enables us to build the correct system of interactions, and to create the conditions for optimally realizing the opportunity we have in this life - to attain the purpose of our creation."

"In order to create efficient and healthy communication with a child, we need to understand that each new generation has new and different values from our own, ones which do not match our expectations. If we ignore this conflict - between parents' aspirations and the new level of the child's development - it will inevitably end in rebellion.

Through the observation of the nature of man, Kabbalists have concluded that the only chance of a child listening to a parent is if he feels he will benefit from taking the advice. Therefore, it is wise to give advice or an explanation that will provide the child with the feeling that by accepting it, he will personally gain something that is not necessarily connected with the parent. That requires a parent to be honest with himself, and to examine the essence of his advice - he must continually ask himself, "Who is this advice actually serving?"

"It is vital for the advice not to appear in the form of 'Do's and Don'ts,' but to cause the child to understand by himself, within himself, what he needs to do. That way, he won't feel that a certain process is being forced upon his life, but will feel that the idea of change developed independently within him."

"To 'love a child' means to separate one's behavior between strictness and love, and to set up a proper contrast of one in regard to the other, building a middle line between them for the benefit of the one at whom it is directed.

The treatment of an adult in regard to a little child is very serious, very difficult, and very intense. It needs to be under constant self-control, which means that the adult needs to be brought up first. He needs to understand what he needs to be like.

From the first days of a child's existence, like a little animal, a child is made to feel the adult, and already properties of the three lines are implanted in him. These reins—the right and the left—will be felt by him subconsciously, instinctively, without having opened his eyes yet, being blind and not hearing anything, like in his first days, but he will understand this nonetheless."

The Father's Role in Educating His Children in Kabbalah

Question:

And is it harmful for a child to participate in the game with the father?

Dr's Answer:

In this case, the purpose of hunting is not provision for life, but an exercise in order to kill, cheat, and prosper at the expense of others. Obviously, these things should be rejected at their very core. From the very beginning, even from before birth—and certainly during the period when the child begins to comprehend things—giving him such games poses a very big problem. He is already coming into this world after previous incarnations, weighed down by the egoistical nature, the growing evil, and the flaming ego. And we must consider the fact that with his development these properties will increase. That is why we must instill correct values in him from the earliest age, so that he is able to cope with his nature.

I remember that in my time, the bringing up of children used to be based on the emphasis for every child to know that he should be good: not to fight with anyone, be kind to all. Why? Because we unconsciously understand that if a person treats all others well, he will end up having fewer enemies, a smaller chance to get into a problematic situation, or provoke a wish in someone to cause him trouble. That is why we should not teach him how to kill others, use them, or pursue them with the intention to cause them harm. On the contrary, teach him how to do good to others. This way, you will be able to provide for him, to an extent, a safer life in the future.

This is what we wish for our children. But to teach our child the opposite - that is to kill, means making him unhappy. Throughout his life he will live under the pressure of the thought that others might treat him that same way. What a powerful inner pressure is awaiting him, and what for? Besides, the destiny of a human soul depends on his treatment of others. The better he treats others, the more he benefits in the end.

Question:

I would like to share my own personal experience of how my son went to school, to the first grade. The initial period of him being there was a cultural shock for us (for him, and as a consequence, for us). He was telling us that the children there were constantly fighting during breaks and were only preoccupied by doing harm to each other. Such was the main pastime of the society. For our daughter, the experience was not the same because girls, by their nature, are gentler. Let's say, a small child, whom we are trying to raise with only kind and positive treatment of others, falls into a society with other values. Wouldn't he turn out to be somewhat of a "wimp," where everyone can beat him and he only smiles in return? Is such a danger present?

Dr's Answer:

You are right. But in the end, I think that in such a way he is not attracting hate towards himself, or the desire to use him. No. The point is, that if he treats others well, it does not mean that he cannot stand for himself. But you are not teaching him, "programming" him, to constantly hunt people, like some kind of a predator animal. My son began to study Kabbalah with me - he was only nine years old then. But at the same time he was studying many things: wrestling, bicycling, and others. That is, I was raising him to be strong, but not for the purpose of using other people and threatening them with his strength. He is strong, and if necessary, or when left with no alternative, he can stand for himself. But in his nature there is no inclination to kill, torment someone, and so on. There must be a balance between these two issues because we live in a very, very cruel world. However, we do not have to be like everyone else.

When Parents Disagree on the Need to Educate Their Children in Kabbalah

Question:

Who is responsible for the upbringing in the family, the man or the woman? And how is this related to the spiritual?

Dr's Answer:

It is written, "Follow the father's morals and mother's Torah." It means that the father is responsible for the morals and the mother, for the Torah, i.e. together. What does it mean, "mother" and "father" in this case, and what is the difference between the morals and Torah? It seems that Torah is the main thing; however, the mother is responsible for it. The father only menaces and gives warnings. Doesn't it seem it's easier?

This implies that the two sides act in harmony on the child who feels their interconnection. One side supposedly has to provide him with problems from his nature that can be awakened in him and dominate. On the other hand, there needs to be a methodology of how to overcome these problems. One can advance in his life by bringing together both of these sides. This means the morals on one side and Torah on the other side reveal to a small child (as well as to a big one since all of us are children) the opportunity to advance by the means of two lines—the right one and left one.

The Best and Most Correct Environment for a Child

"Kabbalists resolutely object to systems that coerce any kind of moral principles on man, especially on children. The reason is that Kabbalah maintains that the development is always personal and internal, defined by the individual himself. The result of it is that man changes for the better outwardly, as well, and has a positive effect on society.

It would be wrong to leave our children completely unattended to because they are still in the general environment that builds them, and not in the right environment that can give them the right atmosphere for inner, spiritual development.

My teacher wrote that one should stay away from any kind of extreme societies, or he will absorb their extreme views and ideas on life.

Because it is impossible to avoid any kind of influence, we must begin educating our children at an early age, in a traditional framework. Such a framework would:

1. Protect them from extreme religious or otherwise secular views.

2. Give the child the perspective of Kabbalah, and its approach to life, to our everyday actions and the knowledge of the meaning of our lives.

Many parents ask me for help. They do not know what to do with their children. The most difficult problem is drugs. It is prevalent in youth from the ages of 14-15 and up, and it is constantly getting worse. A high percentage of high school students are on drugs today.

From the point of view of Kabbalah it is best to:

1. Send the children to high-level schools, where they can get a good matriculation certificate.

2. Distance the children from a bad influence of a social environment, such as one infected with drugs and other critical perversions.

3. The child should feel an inner freedom of choice, yet on the outside he should still feel the limits of public opinion and the strength of his parents."

Question:

So I am allowed to choose the environment for my child, because I chose so?

Dr's answer:

You have to, it's not that you are allowed to or not. You are obliged to do so, because you are on the path, and you are already holding on to the goal. You are obliged to pass this on to the child. Whether you want to or not, you are giving him some kind of upbringing. So you should pass on to him the kind of upbringing, which you have chosen, which you see as correct.

You shouldn't pass on to him the type of upbringing in which you do not believe, to which you do not belong. But when you do belong to such upbringing, you have to give it to him, as you generally have to give a child what he needs.

Question:

And where can I not interfere with what is called child's inner part?

Dr's Answer: There is no part in a child in which you cannot interfere because the child is under your power, he is subjected to you. He is not called a stranger; he exists under your power. That is, your duty is to give him an upbringing that you choose, even if against his will. You most probably choose a certain form of upbringing. Even if you don't choose anything, he feeds on some type of a society. That is why we are obligated to give our upbringing to the children, as much as it is possible, the same method. So we must organize a method and build it for all ages of the young generation.

In lieu of an optimum environment for a child, how can the influence of the general society be mitigated?

Question:

I have a question regarding upbringing. When and where can a parent force a child to do something, and when he cannot do so?

Dr's Answer:

Besides being limited by the state laws, it would also be correct to limit them by the laws of nature given in the Torah. If you take all the laws from the Torah about relating to children, friends, neighbors, the state, the world, you will see how to relate to things because the laws of the Torah are the laws of nature. This way, you can deduct the laws regarding behavior, the relationship between a person and friends, a person and family, and according to that understand what is going on.

It is written regarding children: Those who do not teach a child a certain profession are making him a robber, a thief. A father is obliged to teach his son the faith, meaning an occupation. What is meant here is that an occupation is explained as faith, meaning craft. "Craft' is described as "faith," that is, according to the structure of the Upper *Partzufim*, *Abba* (father) should educate his child so that based on this education, a child could reach *Katnut*, *Gadlut* in his inner *Kelim*. This is your obligation. It's not that you can or cannot; you are obliged.

Question:

Let's take an example: We choose the environment; I choose which environment to be in, even on the simplest level.

Dr's Answer:

It is because you are in the transitional state between the generations, because you are the first generation that searches for the truth and finds it from the point in the heart. The next generation, they will come, just like you, who receive this spark in their hearts in the middle of their lives (they searched, and they came to the corrections). Or those will come, who were born into families, already on the path. And those who are already on the path, must pass on such upbringing to the children. The child has no freedom of choice in this.

"Our children understand that to leave the society, the circle of interests, the knowledge, talks, and discussions, and to generally reject the life that Kabbalists, their parents, lead, for the sake of life in the regular world, means to simply fall into a grey abyss. Although, of course, as all young people, they try to get something from our external world, but its emptiness drives them back. We see this. In addition, for the sake of fairness we should note that we do not force Kabbalistic upbringing on our children in any way; there is not even a trace of this, and this did not exist even in my time. That is, they simply observe how we live and hear our conversations; after all, our children sometimes come with us to different gatherings and events, such as weddings and dinners, where all members of our families are present. As a rule, this turns out to be sufficient. The process of upbringing happens of its own accord, unintentionally. A child simply sees, hears and absorbs the example that the parents give, and this is enough for him to at least not go after drugs, the way we see this everywhere today in all Israeli schools. Our example is enough to prevent them from bad actions; we can say this about girls as well as boys."

"Each of us strives to give his or her children the best tools for life. This is why we intuitively bring them up to be altruists. In fact, educating the younger generation has always been based on altruistic values.

We bring our children up to be kind to others because we subconsciously know that being unkind to others eventually hurts the unkind person. We want to give our children security, and we feel that we can succeed only by means of altruistic education.

Thus, a person's confidence does not depend on the individual, but on the environment. Because one's environment reflects a person's attitude toward it, all harm comes to us from the environment. However, by promoting altruistic values, we will increase the chances that society will not harm us.

Each society, in each country, throughout history, has wanted to impart altruistic values to its children. Only a very powerful individual, such as a tyrant whose army stands ready to enforce his will, can afford to teach his children to be ruthless, inconsiderate, and merciless. But the children of such people will need great protection to survive. They will have to stand guard against everyone else, and protect themselves through the force of arms.

A good attitude toward others imparts a sensation of security, peace and calm that is second to none. For this reason, we try to bring up our children with these values. However, and this is an important point, in time our children see that we, ourselves, are not behaving in this way toward others, and so they become as egoistic as we are.

Proper education is based on good examples. Are we showing our children an example of altruistic behavior toward others? The answer is probably negative, although we do bring them up to be altruistic when they are young. A child who sees that his or her parents do not "walk the walk, but simply talk the talk," senses that their words are empty and false. As much as they will try to show children the honorable way to behave, it will be useless.

The crises we are in today, and our perilous future, impel us to make a change. Thus far, we have been teaching our children to do one thing, yet without following our own advice. But now we have no choice. We must change our own egoistic attitude toward others.

As more and more people begin to behave altruistically, the reality that our children will be born into will change, and they will easily grasp what was difficult for us to understand.

They will recognize that we are all part of a single system, and that accordingly, our relationships should be altruistic. There is nothing better that we can do for our children and for ourselves."

Should a Child Be Isolated or Sheltered in Any Way?

"...[T]here is no coercion in spirituality. It is a key rule. One must choose freely. It is not a coincidence that many of the children of some of the greatest Kabbalists never touched Kabbalah. After all, the desire for spirituality is not hereditary."

"The same applies for the upbringing of children. There must be no pressure, if you don't want, don't do. You can only set an example from which your children can learn. But if you teach them right, you should not say no to them."

"Some rules we learn from experience, some rules of behavior children pick up from their parents, their friends, the environment, and the general society. The rules we learn by education are not innately known to us. It is not clear that this is how they actually exist in the world, but our educators persuade us in various ways that it is so, and that this is a path worth treading. If children could see for themselves that something was wrong, they would not do it."

Group

Women's Desire Leads

Question:

You have often said that a man does what a woman wants, whether he wants to or not. Do men globally influence the desire of women?

Answer:

The female desire is the desire to receive, and the male desire is the desire to bestow. The male desire and the female desire exist in each of us, and we also know that according to our chromosomes.

Therefore, it is natural that the men's groups and the women's groups are also divided into the male and female parts. In every group the desire to receive and the desire to bestow are revealed in a different manner, and we have to use them correctly.

Women are more organized, more dedicated, and committed than men. They constitute the foundation of our world. A man, however, carries out the woman's desire. If we allow the women in the group to have a greater influence in the group, then I am sure that the groups will be more united, more serious, and more purposeful.

The Most Reliable Thing in the World

Question:

What is the influence of the women's group on the men's group? Where can women get the desire to have an impact on men?

Answer:

A few years ago I was in Chile where there are many more women than men. I remember I asked a couple, our friends from the Chilean group, "Who commands at your home?" The husband answered, "Of course, when we are in public, in the street, at a party, then of course, the woman. But at home...!" The wife looked at him like at a small child, nodded a few times, and everything became clear.

This is given by nature that the woman commands everywhere. And that is correct. That is good.

That is why the women's part of the group is the most reliable thing that exists in life and in the world. It is stability, balance, very strong support. And that is why it is necessary first of all to take care that the women's group is strong. It is necessary to give women the opportunity to live, work, and take part in everything. Women's voices must be taken into consideration when making decisions. A good future of the general group lies in this.

We are all adults and understand how impossible it is to be alone, how much we need support. And just because we are different, we reach the right decision and correct life. So, it is necessary to solve the problem seriously, like adults. The women's part of the group should be no less right than the men's part.

The Thin Line between Male and Female Work

Question:

How can women feel the collective descent and unity? I don't feel any descents; I come to the group with great happiness and devote myself to it. So where is my spiritual development?

Answer:

There is something unique among women in comparison to men. It is not required of them to overcome their natural barrier between them. But in the spiritual work, they must be like the men.

Nobody requires them to; nobody demands of them the same method of connection as it is with the men. But inwardly, they are ready for this and must work on it especially between them.

And afterward, both a particular detachment and ascent are created, and the sensation that you are a woman and this is a man disappears. When this outer envelope disappears, and becomes unimportant, then on one hand, what will remain is the physical world, and on the other hand, the spiritual world. Both of them will be precisely differentiated, our beastly nature and that of the soul, then they will be able to work like the men.

But until that moment there is a difference between men and women; therefore, we need to rise and desire spiritual attainment separately. Certainly, we need to help each other in everything, but if we begin to work together, then we only become confused. We confuse images from the physical world and spiritual work, and the outcome is very bad.

Therefore, in no way must we intersect in a serious way. Mutual help, supporting the center, dissemination, everything else is done together, except for spiritual work. Sometimes even the workshops can be jointly arranged. But in general, connection needs to be differentiated according to gender.

You understand and feel this, that you yourselves can easily become confused. Moreover, the women get more confused than the men. A man understands what he needs, whereas a woman confuses spirituality with materialism. For her it is as if it is the same thing. And this is not at all so. She is simply lying to herself without understanding and feeling this.

When you pass through the *Machsom* and really begin to feel the Upper World, you will then understand how much this would have been a mistake. But until then, you will be unable to. Therefore, with us everything is strictly divided into masculine and feminine parts.

Don't interfere with the men; this is the first condition. Second, learn among yourselves. Nobody calls upon you to hug. Do everything that is beneficial for your connection.

Don't Confuse the Spiritual with the Physical

Question:
What are the perfect relationships between men and women in the group?

Answer:
The perfect relationship is the mutual yearning to unite only our desires for the Creator and not any other desires. It is best if we don't pay attention to the bodies. It doesn't matter who I am dealing with, whether it is a man or a woman, but if it disturbs me, I should make it so that it doesn't disturb me. In fact, in the spiritual world the male and the female desires exist in each of us.

There is a desire to receive, AHP, and a desire to bestow, GE. This means that in the spiritual world things don't take place the way they do in our world in the corporeal bodies. There, only the desires connect, the desires for the Creator and no other desires; all the other desires are egoistic, and therefore they don't exist in spirituality.

If a person wants to eat two meals for lunch, he should go ahead, since it doesn't stand in the way of his spiritual advancement. If he likes a certain girl, then it doesn't interrupt his spiritual advancement either. What's important is what his main desire is focused on. If it is focused on the Creator, everything else becomes part of that.

The relationships between men and women in the group should be regulated and organized so that they don't interrupt the spiritual advancement in any way.

Question:

Suppose that I can hug my friend as a man, but I cannot picture myself doing it correctly with women.

Answer:

Your relationships with women should be established so that they don't interfere with spiritual advancement, so that the spiritual and the physical are not confused. Spiritual is spiritual, and physical is physical.

High Hopes

Question:

What do you expect from the women in their convention and from their mutual preparation with the men for the Arava Convention?

Answer:

I expect a lot from the women because it is the principle part of our world group. The fact is that the women are much more modest than the men; they are very active, but they stay at the back, on the sidelines.

Women's help is limitless, but all the fruits of their efforts they quietly give to the men. That is the nature of woman. One needs to note that in this they are certainly closer to bestowal than men. Women do a lot, even though we don't feel it. Thus, I honor their work and am very happy about their cooperation and participation.

Besides that, in all of our worldwide groups, the number of women is not less than the men, and that is a huge force. Now, when humanity is beginning to gradually move to a new state that isn't familiar to it, the women's participation is especially important.

We need their desire, the yearnings, and their pressure on the men. We need to make them even more active so that they will pressure us, like a wife to her husband who is under her constant supervision. It is very important that a man feels that his wife values his spiritual work and follows after him, pushes him, understands what he is involved with, and controls him. It gives a man meaning and directs him.

We must feel this, and then we will be able to better advance forward. Thus, on the one hand, we must divide our work and part of our events to men and women. But on the other hand, we must encourage the woman's part to connect, to unite, to work together, and give them every opportunity to share one huge powerful desire that will force us to realize it.

No Development without Women

With women everything is assessed by the degree to which they desire to be together and support or surround the male part. Women have to put pressure on the men. This is their character. They must only use it truly correctly, without being embarrassed. Women depend on the men's group, and it depends on them. The men's group will not move forward without women.

The female inclination is primary, while the male inclination is secondary. That is how all of nature is built. If it weren't for women, men would spend their whole lives playing soccer. Yet the female inclination forces them to create a family, to work, to come home, and arrange something. All of this is the female desire, not the male one. A man does not have any of this. He is like a child his whole life.

That is why women have to get organized the right away and put pressure and influence on the men. And the men have to understand this. We are adults and we have to use our nature, both the female and the male, in order to attain the goal. The goal is attained mutually. It is like the birth of a new baby that belongs to both.

Therefore, you should look at this seriously and mutually. It isn't a coincidence that we were created precisely this way. We look at everything as an accidental occurrence, but in reality we must collect everything inside of us to the maximum and combine it the right way. Then we will acquire a desire in which the Creator will be revealed. Nothing can be done here without the female inclination.

The world consists of 60% women, and they are the most stable half in the world. Similarly, the group is absolutely unstable without the female part. A strong women's group is the guarantee for a stable men's part. It is more stable. By acting correctly, it softens and cushions all the problems, all of the swaying of our common ship.

Women have to understand this and clearly carry out their function. Men also have to understand this and give women the appropriate opportunities, as well as value them. Without this, they won't achieve anything. The male part will immediately "go awry" without the female part. The presence of women suppresses all of the glitches.

Even Abraham was told, "Listen to what Sarah will tell you." The women's basis in development is initially the most important. The entire desire that we have to correct is the female desire, which is expressed through a woman. Therefore, you should organize yourselves the right way. Wherever there is a strong female part, you are guaranteed great success.

Behind Every Successful Man There Is a Woman

Question:

Should women act as if men already are in the quality of **Lishma** *(altruistic intention)?*

Answer:

No! Women should not think that men already are on such a level. They must view them as children. All of us are participating in this game together. They treat men as a mother treats her children and as a wife who sends her husband off to work.

They say that there is a woman behind every successful man, and this is really true. It cannot be any other way. So we want to be some lucky men!

One Global Woman and One Global Man

I see the coming conventions, "One Global Woman" and "A Flame in the Desert," as one convention and I do not differentiate between them. After all, the women's convention is the preparation without which the men's convention cannot succeed.

I am coming there in order to organize the desire, the mutual yearning, the female pressure. One woman should help the other to build this enormous desire for the spiritual birth and pass it on to the men for the convention in the desert. Every man should relate to the woman's convention as essential women's work, thanks to which our home and our family life exist.

We have to help in every way we can to create the conditions for the women's convention to succeed and turn into a real blow and breakthrough to unity. I warn the global men's group that if anyone treats this obligation disrespectfully, it will cause great harm.

Who Smoothes Conflicts in the Group?

Question:

What is the most critical point in the group work when friends' egoism breaks out in the group?

Answer:

I think that here women should go to the forefront. When there are serious problems between men, women should subtly try to smooth the conflict, to indicate, as a mother to a child, that all this is temporary, that these relations are manifested between them on purpose and they should not be carried away, like children, and forget about the cause, while being entangled in the consequences.

If it happens that men are not in a position to resolve a conflict themselves, then the women help them.

On the other hand, men should restrain women if they start criticizing each other, gossiping and slandering.

Men, Do Not Underestimate the Desire of Women!

Question:

How important for spiritual advancement are the physical actions of women in a group?

Answer:

They are 100% important because nobody can take physical actions from you. All your thoughts are self-deception. All that you transfer through the head or the heart is total ego, the physical actions are real actions.

Invest yourselves even though you have no feelings or negative feelings. Show everyone through your actions and deeds that the goal is important to you, so others around you must see this! This is very important! Tell them that you want to see that they are purposeful because you depend upon them.

Question:

I said this, but they don't listen.

Answer:

In that case, I must turn to the men: The desires of women are like this, the yearnings are like that, we must not take advantage under any circumstances!

If you reject the desire of a woman, you need to realize that you won't attain anything. I say this with complete seriousness! We learn this from the correspondence between *"Zeir Anpin"* and *"Malchut."* If, as representatives of *"Partzuf Zeir Anpin,"* you reject the desires of *"Malchut,"* then what kind of serious attainment can you be talking about?! Nothing will succeed for you!

You must feel the desire of women and what women expect from you very acutely! You need to expect this pressure because it is specifically the desire of women, called *"Mei Nukvin,"* which is essential for ascent!

Therefore, if men "don't listen," this is very bad and is the most severe accusation that can be directed at them, and not only from women.

Women's Participation Is Crucial

Question:

If the realization of evil occurs due to the lack of unity, then how does a woman experience this realization if she doesn't do any practical work in uniting? How exactly should she feel unity?

Answer:

This is just like within a family. How can you explain the entire family life in detail and what the relationship between the husband and wife means?

A man and a woman are two images that compose all of humanity, and together they have to create the image of a single soul. This is why the group must consist of men and women, who then have to unite in their work and mutual support.

There should never be any insistence if a husband or a wife does not wish to partake in this. There is no coercion is spirituality; therefore, there shouldn't be any pressure. But in the group the mutual help from both sides should resemble simple family dynamics.

Without women, it's impossible to advance because they are the carriers of natural desire and, therefore, are closer to nature. Without men, it's also impossible to advance since they're the conductors of this Upper energy that's passed on to the female part. It means that we depend on each other in our spiritual development, just as we do in our corporeal life.

Our connection in the group should be like a connection in the correct family unit, where we complete each other. We already see families in all parts of the world where the wife, the kids, and the husband are all taking part in this process. We're organizing virtual schools.

I would like for the women to be a lot more active. I don't understand why the women's part of the groups suddenly quiets down, becomes less active, and exists along with the men but slightly beneath them. I don't understand this.

I have many women helping me with translations and with processing the materials. I have more faith in them than I do in men because women are more devoted to their work and they won't let you down. For this reason, the women's group should be "heard" more.

The Mother's Way

Question:
Is there a difference between man and woman in spirituality?

Answer:
No. In each one of us there are two parts: female and male, and with them we advance. However, with respect to the unity in the group, the male and female souls are a little different in their approaches. Women unite according to their strength, whereas men must connect and unite with all their hearts, in the strongest brotherly bonds.

Here, the entire matter is the uniqueness of the soul: The male soul belongs more to GE (*Galgalta ve Eynaim*) and the female to the AHP (*Awzen, Hotem, Peh*). But both of these need to attain the most upper level, and along the women's way, there are no special obstacles.

I very much suggest to and ask the women to worry about the men, push them to unite and connect, stand in a circle surrounding them in order to prevent them from withdrawing. After all, the men stay as children all their lives. They don't have the mechanism of giving birth and worrying about others. He doesn't change, only grows in size.

On the other hand, when a woman becomes a mother, she goes through very serious hormonal changes in one way or another. In her is concealed the same potential, the same longing, the same understanding. Thus, she is more connected to life, to nature. She is more logical, more realistic. The ups and downs touch her less than they do a man, since her body is used to "swallowing" these blows regularly.

This is the reason that women need to help the men, and this is spoken about a lot in the wisdom of Kabbalah. Without the help of women, the men won't attain the goal. So take care of them like mothers who cherish their babies.

Wiping Out the Differences in Spiritual Work

Question:

*What is **Arvut** (Mutual Guarantee) from the stand point of a woman? Is it support and raising the importance of the goal?*

Answer:

Since the world has begun to discover the general crisis, there is no difference between men and women as far as attaining the Upper World, in the work between them. Women also sit in workshops and participate in them just like the men, and they experience the same feelings no less than the men. So, I don't think that there is any difference between the men and women.

It seems to me that all of that is gradually disappearing. All the previous differences will become more internal. This means that within each one of us there are two lines, a man and a woman, and we need to join them again into one common line, in that same *Adam* (human) that was created, not as a man or a woman, but as it included both from the start, it is understood that both the nature of the man and the woman operates in him.

When Rabash began to write his articles, he gave them to the women's group, and the women read and discussed them. This means that he was concerned about how they would perceive them.

In the time of Rabash, we had to enlarge the room made especially for the women where they attended and listened to our classes three times. I am convinced that nowadays, there is no problem with the presence of women in their support and their active and equal participation with the men. I simply don't see any special differences, and with the years, we will see less and less. But in the places where the men connect and hug, there is no place for women, but this is because these disturbances exist in us.

And if the roundtables are arranged side-by-side, even in the same room, or in two different rooms, it is only so that we won't be distracted on the corporeal level, so as not to disturb us. And so, there is no difference. I personally don't feel inside that there is a difference. And besides that, I hear women's responses in the workshops that we organize on Sundays and see how much they understand the essence and how much they grasp everything that happens, no less than the men. So, there is no need to pay attention to this.

We need to differentiate between women and men only in one thing. Entering the women's organization and working in it is only for women. With all other things, there shouldn't be a separation.

The Unity of the World Lies in Harmony between Men and Women

We should never perceive the relationship between men and women as antagonistic. On the contrary, we have to see each other as help. If we are talking about the unity of the world, then first of all this is the mutual support of its two parts—male and female.

These parts come from the common root of creation: the Creator or Light, and the desire or the vessel filled with Light. In addition, this vessel goes through all sorts of forms as it changes. And inside of this vessel, both of us—the male and the female parts—have to work together integrally, like in an ideal family.

The common, collective image of the man has to work together with the common, collective image of the woman. They must work together conjointly, mutually, and clearly, each understanding the nature of both. A man understands himself and the female nature, while a woman understand herself and the male nature, and together we act sensibly and wisely, as educated, serious adults who aspire toward a common goal.

The goal is attained through the connection between us. It is written, "Man and woman, and the Creator between them." That is to say, the Creator's revelation takes place precisely in the right connection between them, on the screen that appears between the Light and the desire. That is how we must complete one another, mutually and constantly. There is no part, no tiny detail, not one phenomenon in nature, in our relationships, in our world and the spiritual worlds, that does not have mutual supplementation, unification, and adhesion of the male and female parts.

In our world this is not apparent at all. We do not even imagine this mutual supplementation, unification, and adhesion. But in the spiritual world, this is a necessary condition. And depending on what levels we are on, these levels are determined precisely by the mutual supplementation and unification, until we unite together.

Therefore, the right understanding of our mutual work is the most important condition of our success. I would say that there is no problem that could be solved separately by men or by women. They are always solved one through the other, meaning that women's problems are solved through men, and men's problems are solved through women. This lack of understanding, the belief that it is possible to exist separately, "What do I care about them!" (usually, this is how men feel about women), and "We will solve everything on our own and will do everything ourselves!" This attitude that men tend to have is completely incorrect. And naturally, on the part of women it is also incorrect to think that "Men will do something, will solve everything, and everything will be OK, and we will receive something by being next to them."

Initially, from the very first step, there has to be clear, inner contact. It shouldn't be external, physical, visual, or even verbal, but precisely inner contact, which occurs through the Upper Force, through the next level, instead of directly between us. Then this upper degree will be expressed inside of this unity. It's like a minus and a plus, and some kind of resistor or device between them that starts working precisely in this way, by virtue of the poles that are connected to it.

Dissemination

Dissemination and Unity

Question:

In all three days of the convention we have said that only dissemination to 99% of humanity will truly help unite the group. Do we unite in order to go out to disseminate, or do we go out to disseminate in order to unite?

Answer:

This takes place reciprocally. If we are not involved with dissemination, then we will have no reason to unite and continue inner work in the group; it will all fade away. But when you begin to work with the others, you will begin to discuss all of this, "give birth" to this, and unify this among you. You must show them everything by your example, that basically, the students make the teacher.

On the other hand, you must give birth within you to whatever you teach them. Therefore, advancement of the individual and advancement of the masses are phenomena that depend upon each other reciprocally. You are for them and they are for you.

Most women truly listen to all the lessons, not only the lessons but also the conversations, "A New Life," and our programs in the Kabbalah Media archive. They read my blog methodically. If all of this did not happen, how could a woman go out, how could she tell the general public what to do? What would she go to them with? You see, this really must be alive inside of her. She needs to live and breathe this. And when she does this, she truly does this wholeheartedly. And when she reaches people, it is truly this preparation that convinces them much stronger than the men. Their preparation to persuade, their power to persuade is much higher than the men.

The woman goes together with the man for most of the work, but in the end of the matter, the persuasion, the discovery, and the explanation is done specifically by her. Many more doors are opened and many more hearts are softened following the persuasion of the women. We need to take this into account.

I truly think that we still don't recognize the power of women. We aren't aware; we don't know how much more they can do than the men in an area. The influence of the man on the woman is like the influence of *Malchut* on *Keter*. She establishes everything. *Shechina*, this is woman; *Malchut*, this is woman. She activates the *Zeir Anpin*, she activates everything.

If we only knew how women can activate the general public... This is a discovery that has not yet been revealed in our world. I say this seriously. This is a discovery that must come from spirituality. If women would go out to really act in their current form, and with all their power knew how to convince the women, not the men, then everything would fall into place before them. The time of the exile of the *Shechina*, the redemption, is the power of the women. This is not the power of the men. Therefore, I ask the women very, very seriously, if a man sits at home while a woman goes out to action, this is desirable. He should stay at home.